COSMOPOLITAN'S SUPER DIETS & EXERCISE GUIDE

by Marcia Seligson and *Cosmopolitan*

COSMOPOLITAN BOOKS / NEW YORK

ACKNOWLEDGMENTS
Many experts contributed to *Cosmopolitan's Super Diets & Exercise Guide,* and we are grateful to all of them. Specifically we wish to thank the following authors for permission to reprint articles that appeared originally in *Cosmopolitan* magazine: "Forbidden Fruit for Indulgent Dieters" © 1965 by Gael Greene. In addition, the following © 1965, 1966, 1967, 1968, 1969, 1971 That Cosmopolitan Girl Library, Inc.: "The British Way of Slimming" by Bonnie Buxton; "This Is How I Take It Off" by George Christy; "Belly Dancing for the Inhibited" by Laura Cunningham; "Debbie Drake's Dance-ercizes" by Debbie Drake; "The Diet Worth Eating For" by Deedee Moore; "The Drinking Girl's Diet" by Liz Rittersporn; "Working Girl's Hamburger Diet" by Mimi Sheraton.

Chart on page 35 from *The All-in-One Diet Annual* by Peter Wyden and Lois Libien, copyright © 1970 by Peter H. Wyden, Inc., by permission of Bantam Books.

COSMOPOLITAN BOOKS
Editorial Director, Helen Gurley Brown
Editor-in-Chief, Jeanette Sarkisian Wagner
Senior Editor, Veronica Geng
Copy Editor, Ellen Tabak
Editorial Assistant, Tiena-Kay Halm

CONTENTS

FOREWORD

You may think someone as skinny as I am has no right introducing a diet book to you. Forget skinny! I am *always* dieting ... this very moment I am surely the hungriest woman in New York. It's true I've never been more than ten pounds overweight (as a teen-ager, for some reason, the old metabolism went crazy) but if I ever let go and ate everything I *wanted* to, my hips would soon be five inches larger ... and they're *already* large enough ... and my dear little arms would look like plump white loaves of French bread. (Why did I have to bring *that* up ... I would *love* some plump white French bread right this minute!)

Now ... the reason I don't balloon up is because, as I already mentioned, I *diet*. And diet simply means eating sensibly ... it's a *lifetime* thing, not an on-again, off-again "cure" like a round of sulfanilamide. And when I say I'm hungry *this* minute, that's not because my lifetime diet (sensible-eating) plan is so hard to take, but because it's now 7:00 P.M. as I write this (I stopped eating gumdrops and caramel-coated marshmallows between meals *long* ago) and so of *course* I'm hungry ... looking forward to a delicious little high-protein dinner!

For the rest of my life I'm sure I'll long for chocolate (especially pure Swiss bittersweet chocolate ... bliss!). And once in a while I will *have* ... along with other "baddies" like fettucini Alfredo and buttered corn muffins ... some Swiss chocolate— but most of the time I'll be "good" and even *enjoy* being "good" because (1) having a nice figure is one of life's pleasures; (2) healthful (sensible) eating really is delicious. You'll *see!*

In this book you are about to read you'll receive more practical help in taking weight off and *keeping* it off than you'd ever imagine possible. On so many things Marcia Seligson and I agree *completely.* I'd been doing many of the things Marcia recommends even *before* I read this book. (Exercise is a big part of my schedule—I'm up to an hour and ten minutes daily. Even though I sometimes feel *glued* to the floor at the end of that time, the net effect is absolutely kilowatts of added energy— plus nonbillowing hips at present!) Also, I virtually exist on high-protein, low-calorie foods—I do like health foods (I've *learned* to like them), and cottage cheese with raw vegetables or fresh fruit is a blessing! Each day—if I've been a *good* calorie-counter— I do allow myself a treat. (Yesterday it was a *perfect* fig from the nearby Arm-and-a-Leg Exotic Foods shop.)

But I've learned so many new things from *Cosmopolitan's Super Diets & Exercise Guide* . . . like how I can lunch at "21" with one of Cosmo's writers and *not* have to fast for the next month . . . how to deal with my psyche mercifully when I fall prey to a dieting lapse (I can go through a can of Blum's Almondettes in one sitting and suffer terrible guilt for *days* afterwards!) . . . how to cook for my husband David and myself when he's on a more rigorous no-carbohydrate regimen than I am . . . and so many more wonderful tips on how to keep a dieting life from being pitiful or boring.

Although I can't speak with personal authority about shedding a great deal of weight, I can say that as Editor of Cosmopolitan, I see nearly every book published that has anything to do with beauty or health, and can't imagine how this one could be better, more complete or sympathetic to the needs of a *real* girl. Just about *every* way to lose is explained so you can pick the one that's *perfect* for you . . . including our fabulous *Yes Yes! No No!* diet plan.

Now, I send you on to Marcia Seligson's introduction, which should inspire you to your quest for thinness immediately! (Marcia shed twenty pounds three years ago, and has *kept* them off. I admire her more than I can say!)

And I raise my glass of Fresca to toast the soon-to-be-svelte you . . . go to it!

Helen Gurley Brown

There are two types of people in the world. Yes, someone is *always* saying, "There are two types of people in the world: those who blah-blah-blah, and those who blah-blah-blah." However . . . two types of people *do* exist in the world. . . . those who are thin— yes, physically, chemically, psychologically, spiritually, intellectually, emotionally, genetically, unalteringly *thin;* and the rest of us, who are *fat.* No matter what we weigh at any given moment of any particular month in our lives (currently I'm 134 pounds, just about right for my 5'7" sturdy, athletic frame) we have Fat Souls. Alas, *I* have an incurably Fat Soul.

What is a "Fat Soul," you ask? It lives in a person who thinks about food too much, in wrong ways, for wrong reasons, and at the worst times. Like when I get depressed over a love affair (sound familiar?), or when an editor has returned an article for extensive revisions, or because I've carelessly ignored my checking-account statements and now my *life* is unbalanced—the first thing I want urgently to do is whip up some linguini in butter sauce, or run out for a Sara Lee chocolate cake and devour the entire thing. If I'm nervous at a fancy, intimidating party, do I drink a little too much? Not a chance. My instincts are to station myself robotlike by the hors d'oeuvres table and nibble unceasingly. A first-impressions-count business lunch, a visit with relatives who make me tense, a weekend locked in my apartment with the typewriter and a deadline, a blind date...all those nervous-making situations are rendered tolerable by the compulsive intake of food. I give myself a chocolate reward for being a good girl, a pasta substitute for not getting what I *really* wanted, a carbohydrate comfy in tight places. *That's* Fat Soul eating. It has nothing to do with hunger, nutrition, or even the heady lust for a sliver of cherry cheesecake. Rather, it's caused by other needs that we try—unsuccessfully—to fill with food.

A story to illustrate Fat and Thin Soulness: I have a close friend, a successful magazine writer, married to an equally successful photographer. Judy weighs 104 pounds. Not only is she devoted to eating, but she talks about food passionately and incessantly, is the best gourmet cook I know, and delivers faultless information on who sells the best croissants in New York, or the runniest Brie. Judy knows what a quenelle is, and a beignet, and a blanquette. I don't know exactly what they are because what I *do* know is that they are lethally fattening and I have never dared order any one of them in a restaurant. She knows what Italian spot has the best zabaglione, while I—I swear to you—have never ended an Italian dinner with anything but unsweetened espresso.

After sailing to Europe first class on the S.S. *France* (dubbed by noted food experts the finest restaurant in the world), where there is not a thing to do all day but eat and the eating is prepaid anyway, where every steward is a latent Jewish Momma who would be so happy if you had just a little more on your plate, Judy disembarked at Le Havre the same 104 minuscule pounds, though she'd consumed at least three whopping meals a day!

Not glands, friends, not glands. Also not an example of the Great Injustice of Life. Judy is simply one of the other kind of people . . . a Thin Soul.

My friend and her sister Thin Souls just don't function the way we do in relation to food. Yes, she eats everything she desires. But she *doesn't* desire that everything eight times a day and in elephantine quantities. She doesn't have to eat six Mary Janes just because a candy dish happens to be in the same room. If she wants an ice cream cone, she needn't have it *this instant*, and as often as not she forgets about it completely after a few minutes. She doesn't always, inevitably, respond to food just because it's *there*. When she's had enough, she stops. You see, Judy eats out of hunger, not when she's anxious or depressed. At those times, she'll do other things: buy a new pair of boots, go to a double feature, seduce her husband. If she's tempted by the chocolate cake, she eats *one piece*. She can devour the zabaglione for dessert while I'm sitting there pretending espresso makes me quiver with delight, because she's had the sense not to put away four slices of bread and butter during dinner. If she's dining on quenelles, she lunches on yogurt, or nothing. You see, there's intelligence at work; moderation and free choice rule her eating habits. (I, on the other hand, am constitutionally incapable of pushing away a plate that still has a morsel of *anything* on it.)

Until a few years ago I was always twenty pounds overweight. Then suddenly at the age of twenty-eight, I lost that fat in nine weeks, and it has never returned. Oh, sure—five pounds over the Christmas holidays, six pounds on vacation in St. Thomas, two during a summer weekend at East Hampton. But I take it off again during the next week or so, and in the summer I'm always pretty thin because the bathing-suit incentive is potent. But alas, I still have a Fat Soul. I always will, and probably so do you or you wouldn't be reading this. However, I've learned to control the excesses of my soul, finally! It's—frankly—an unending battle. I win some skirmishes, lose others. But it's possible, and worth it, to try. This book will help you.

How? Well, under somebody-or-other's ancient theory that Knowledge Is

Power, we'll explore how you get the way you are; that is, Why You Are Fat—your childhood habits, current hangups about eating. We'll teach you—quickly, simply, but *once and for all*—the facts about nutrition and how your body works in regard to food. We'll talk a lot about the role your fat *head* plays, and how to change it. Then, we'll tell you how to take off the blubber, every last unwanted superfluous ounce, with a selection of super diets for you to choose from, the trimmiest exercises, everything you've ever wanted to know about calories, how to live a diet life in the real world. Perhaps most crucial of all, we'll help you keep it off forever. (If you've *ever* dieted in your life, you know that this part is stickiest.) We've even included a fabulous Dieter's Gourmet Cookbook, and a detachable calorie-counter-plus-daily-diary—not for your innermost secret jottings, but to record every day's food intake and weekly weight loss.

A few words about what this book will *not* do. It will not kid you into thinking that dieting is the most fabulously entertaining and exciting activity in life. Dieting is a drag. The really best foods are either sweet and gooey and deadly fattening, or heavy and filling and deadly fattening. There is no way I can convince you that a plate of broccoli is more seductive and satisfying than a plate of ravioli, or that a celery stalk will make you happy. A celery stalk will never make you the slightest bit ecstatic, nor will cottage cheese. Not the way a hot fudge sundae does. That's the truth.

The other thing I won't do is give you one rigid, supposedly stupendous diet to follow. What I *will* give you is a score of diets that you can choose from, and—if you don't like any of those—instructions for creating the perfect diet for *you*. You see, I believe the only way a diet can really work is if it's tailored specifically to *your* personal, idiosyncratic needs and cravings. Do you loathe fish? Then why should you force yourself to eat fish five times a week because that's the diet some author decides is best? The perfect diet is the one that's most alluring, appetizing, and fulfilling for you alone. You're the one who'll be living with it.

One more bit of information about me. For the first twenty-five years of my life there were only four foods in the world that I *didn't* worship—liver, whipped cream, mushrooms, and jelly doughnuts. Then one night a few years ago at a dinner party I discovered I adored whipped cream. So there you are. It's never easy.

Marcia Seligson

PART ONE

WHY ARE YOU SO FAT?

CHAPTER 1: LAND OF CREAM AND HONEY

There's no question about it, we're a country of Fat Souls. Depending on whose statistics you read—insurance companies', federal agencies', women's magazines', other diet books'—75 to 100 million Americans (or fifty-eight percent of the total population) and three out of five Americans over forty (or *sixty* percent of *them*) are overweight. One expert claims that 10 million of us are on a diet at any given time; all agree that women have greater weight difficulties than men.

I took my own informal survey a few weeks ago by strolling up Madison Avenue from Forty-second to Fifty-seventh Street (the core of smart, busy, well-dressed Manhattan), counting figures that seemed too well padded, from those with five pounds of unnecessary thigh emerging from velveteen hot pants to those who deserved the label "obese." (Incidentally, "overweight" means up to twenty percent *over* desirable body weight; "obese" is beyond *that*.) I was shocked to discover that, according to my count, more than half of the people I scanned seemed too fat. More than one out of every two.

Try the same test in London's Piccadilly Circus or at the Prado in Madrid, and I bet you a sack of gumdrops you'll be astonished to notice how thin the people are. O.K., you say smugly, but look at the

Italians: All that fettucine Alfredo and spaghetti carbonara . . . why we're a nation of Miss Universes compared to the folks in Pastaland, right? Wrong. *We* are the *fattest* country on the planet.

Why? Probably because we are the most affluent nation on the earth, and prosperity—fortunately and unfortunately—is inextricably linked to food. The Good Life . . . well-being . . . several chickens in every pot . . . the bulging refrigerator next to the self-defrosting freezer. Millions of Americans clearly remember the Depression, with its bread lines, constant, gnawing hunger, fear of disease and starvation. "Never Again" is the unspoken slogan, and thus the United States has become, in the past thirty-five years, utterly food-obsessed.

Take, as a single example, the remarkable supermarkets in Los Angeles. Open twenty-four hours a day, many of them are as vast, colorful, joyous, and full of fantasy as Disneyland: constant canned music, a produce area comparable in size to the Hollywood Bowl, endless shelves of consumer goods (including liquor and clothing) designed specifically to enhance your life. Ralph's Supermarket on Sunset and La Brea is one of the Hollywood spots *guaranteed* to contain movie stars. (I once spied Kirk Douglas buying a pork roast.) My friend Beverly reports that she stops at Ralph's several times a week merely to buy a container of sour cream and some soap flakes, invariably emerging forty-five minutes later, eleven dollars poorer, and in a semihypnotic trance. The American supermarket is overwhelming, irresistible.

Another example of wretched excess: The franchised "fast foods" restaurants continue to spread like poison ivy. (Why, Colonel Sanders is practically a bigger household word than Dr. Reuben.) The landscape from New York to California is one long hallucination of fried chicken, pizza, ice cream, and triple burgers. One could easily eat nothing but these four items during a ten-day coast-to-coast drive. Why has nobody started a chain of *diet* eateries?

Affluence also gives people more leisure, which accounts for the gourmet cooking boom of recent years. The video chef Julia Child whips up some unpronounceable miracle on coast-to-coast TV, wipes her chubby hands on her apron, and we *know* we can do it too. Women in Minneapolis chop ginger root and bamboo shoots in their weekly Mandarin cooking class. Magazines explode with recipes, hints for entertaining, and ads for fabulous new kitchen equipment. A Brazilian restaurant opens in Phoenix. You can buy more than thirty books on Chinese cooking. My sixteen-year-old cousin Carl returns from a hiking trip through Europe and bugs his mother to cook him a cassoulet.

Yes, food has become a success symbol: The more our wallets expand, the more, apparently, do our waistlines. Why the connection? For one thing, we just eat wrong. An illustrative statistic: The average American consumes a hundred pounds of sugar a year, nearly all of which provides what nutritionists call "empty calories"—calories that add almost nothing (like commercial soft drinks) to our life-sustaining processes.

Another reason for increasing portliness: The physiological fact is that we get fatter as we get older. Body tissue is constantly being replaced by fat—even if we don't gain any pounds on the scale. Then, too, Americans are getting more sedentary—to the point where inactivity is practically a national characteristic! Why isn't all this leisure we've been raving about spent on the tennis courts or paddling a canoe? No, no—the majority of us use this newfound nonwork time to commute (we've moved to the sub-urbs and bought a second car, so now it takes longer to get to our jobs!), or to collapse in front of the tube. And while we're exerting less and less energy (i.e., burning *fewer* calories), we're "noshing" more. I find it physically impossible to spend more than one hour catatonic in front of the TV without becoming ravenously hungry. The desire has nothing to do with *appetite* in any real sense—it's more like boredom, a vague, growing fatigue, the inability to *really* relate to television, the need to move some part of my body actively, be it only the *mouth!*

Do all these theories explain why anywhere from 40 to 100 million people are too fat? Does it describe why *you* have weight hangups? I eat like a sparrow, you insist, and I just *can't* lose an *ounce!* I look at my friends who are skinny and devour *everything*, you plead, while I gain weight from chewing on an ice cube. *What about my glands?*

If you truly believe your weight problems are glandular, you must put this book down right now and make a doctor's appointment for a complete check-up, including basal metabolism and endocrine tests. When he tells you that you do *not* have an underactive thyroid or *anything else physiological* that prevents you from shedding bulk—when he tells you that, and *you are utterly convinced*—come back and read on. For the tough truth is that *hardly anybody is fat because of glandular disturbances*. We are fat because we eat too much of the wrong things! Accept that.

CHAPTER 2: CHECK YOUR PAST

Another common argument to the "We are fat because we eat too much" thesis is heredity. My next-door neighbor Avery is a hefty 225-pounder who rides up and down the scale like an elevator. He insists the reason he can't lose thirty pounds and *keep it off* is heredity. "My mother is overweight, my father, my sister, my sister's children, my cousins in Detroit, and my uncle Sidney. It runs in my family, that's all. I just have to live with it."

Avery, you're a _____! Indeed, obsesity *does* tend to run in families. (A recently conducted study in England showed that less than ten percent of children with normal weight had parents who were overweight.) But there is *no* conclusive scientific evidence to indicate that genes, not *eating habits*, are at fault. It is a true, bona fide *cop-out* to believe that you are doomed to plumpness forever because cousin Paulette in Beverly Hills owns the same fifteen extra pounds that run in the family. Yes, almost surely Paulette's weight and yours *are* related— because her mother and yours are sisters, come from the same environment, and developed the same *unhealthy eating patterns*—nutritionally *and* psychologically—which they passed on to you and cousin Paulette. Got that?

For us Fat Souls, eating has *very little* to do with its intended functions: to nourish the body, aid in physical growth and health, and provide a pleasurable *periodic* activity. *We* use food for a myriad of *other* purposes, even ignoring those few basic functions. (Think about the fatties we *all* know who can't tell a protein from a golf ball.) And chances are, we've been at this unsavory *misuse* of food for most of our lives.

`Picture a tiny, gurgling baby, a little bundle, and think about whether you've ever said while cooing over that infant, "Oh, he's so fat!" What we mean is he's obviously loved, well cared for, and happy because he's a *chubby* baby instead of a lean one. And his mother thinks she is giving him her love because he is growing plumper daily.

That's where it all starts, the Food Equals Love Syndrome—the notion that soft, sweet foods equal security. Now, much of the equation *is* realistic: An infant *is* nourished and sustained by his mother, and this is his primary need as a baby. But as he grows, Momma transfers to the Candy Syndrome: "You were *such* a good girl, Marcia, I'm going to give you a special treat." And what's the treat? A chocolate something or a marshmallow gooey. Not a book or a toy or a trip to the zoo, but *something to eat*. A reward, a surprise, perhaps a teeny blackmail. ("If you make all the beds, I'll bake you some cookies.") It's *always sweet!* I never heard of a kid being offered a slice of halibut for being good. Also, from childhood on, celebrations are invariably linked to food. Remember your first toddler party? The highlight of the day was *not* the games, the fun, the being with your pals, but the ice cream and cake.

Let's take a mini-trip back to your childhood to get some idea of where your current eating habits began. Think about your family's patterns: What particular foods were the favorites, prepared most often? How big were the portions? How often did you eat? What about snacks?

In my family it was customary to eat meat for breakfast (I never tasted cereal until my first day in the college dormitory) as well as for dinner and many lunches; so today steak and hamburgers are still my passion fruits. Nobody craved desserts, but the portions of beef, vegetables, and potatoes were gargantuan; then somehow a sandwich, or cheese and crackers, magically appeared three hours after dinner in the middle of homework or television. To reject my mother's juicy roast-beef sandwiches would not only have been humanly *impossible*, but would deeply have wounded this slaving woman who spent *every* waking instant catering to what *she imagined* were the children's needs.

My friend Nancy, always ten pounds overweight, totally uninterested in anything but carbohydrates, traces her hangups back to the childhood meals she made for herself while her parents were at work. She existed on peanut-butter-and-jelly sandwiches, pretzels, doughnuts—anything filling and *easy* to grab. Today, she admits, she would happily thrive on peanut-butter-and-jelly sandwiches, with some canned macaroni and cheese thrown in for nourishment!

Tom's mother, a thin-obsessed California beauty, constantly besieged her children about weight, so his adolescent rebellion—instead of taking the form of long hair or smashing the family Ford—fixated on cream puffs and malteds. He's still battling the waistline.

If *your* mother opened the refrigerator door a hundred times a day to toss a morsel of cheese, a cracker, or a handful of grapes into her mouth, probably *you* do the same thing now and can't understand why you're chubby when you eat such *tiny meals*. In my family—as in many who were Depression-poor and then prospered—feeling hunger at *any* time was traumatic. We were psychologically programmed to dive for the kitchen the instant we felt the slightest twinge of appetite. (Notice how we use the words "appetite" and "hunger" interchangeably, although one literally means a pleasant sensation and the other a nagging deprivation.)

A stocky boyfriend once told me that when he was a teen-ager, being heavy gave him a sense of power, a feeling that he could compete athletically with stronger boys. In my adolescence, fat was just another entry in my Nightmare Catalog—along with pimples, too-curly hair, braces, and the terrible fear that someone would try to kiss me. Or *wouldn't*.

The only refuge was to meet my friends (who of course had precisely the *same* miseries) and gorge ourselves on every known dietary menace. Self-destructive, natch, but so comforting, and (to me) the only gratifying substitute for not being beautiful, popular, happy, confident. *Aha, remember that!* Overeating substitutes for all the things missing from our lives.

CHAPTER 3: IGNORANCE IS FAT

When I went on a major diet program several years ago (I'd been on and off diets since I was seventeen, but somehow knew this time it was for real), I discovered an astonishing thing: I was shockingly ignorant about food. Of course I was aware of the difference between a carrot and a Boston cream pie. Who isn't? But as a compulsive dieter, I assumed I knew everything about the caloric values of foods. Wrong. And I suspect that you, too, may be vastly misinformed—or less informed than you think. I had never been aware, for instance, that the very highest-calorie foods per average portion are beef, pork, and lamb! Not chocolate mousse or whipped potatoes, but those boring little hamburger patties that I felt so virtuous about gobbling every time I started down the highway to thindom. Same with yogurt, advertised as *the* yummy answer to the dieting chore. What the ads somehow never mention is that *any flavored* yogurt contains syrup and sugar—260 calories a cup. Jell-O is a villain, too. (Jell-O, you shriek? Why, I *exist* on Jell-O. Are you thin, dear?) The list is endless: Some foods are much worse than we've ever imagined, and happily, some are much, much better.

   Don't feel guilty about your ignorance. When a survey on nutrition was done in England, sixty percent of the participants didn't know the difference between a vitamin and a calorie. Don't feel guilty, but *do* learn the truth about calories. I don't mean how many calories in a single mushroom, but whether vanilla ice cream, ice milk, or milk sherbet is the *least* fattening; which commonly eaten diet foods are *monsters;* and what *goodies* you can devour in unlimited quantities. Counting calories is boring and compulsive, but a thorough knowledge of what goes into your mouth is critical.

Do you really pay attention to nibbles? When you think you've dieted strenuously for a week and the scale needle hasn't budged, is it perhaps because you didn't notice the entire dish of peanuts you polished off in that bar? Or, though you were careful to order tomato juice while your date had gimlets, did you get so involved in a debate about women's lib that you automatically reached into the corn-chip bowl over and over again, never quite letting those gestures register in your consciousness? For a week or so keep a written record of every single morsel that finds its way to your face—*everything*—and you may be surprised. I *never* eat bread in a restaurant, but when I gave myself the keeping-a-record test, I uncovered the fact that I munch on two or three breadsticks instead. *Without realizing it*.

Now let's talk about portions. As I mentioned, I grew up eating gigantic quantities of *healthful* foods, so my particular problem is to refrain from polishing off five lamb chops or one and a half pounds of steak at a sitting. Until I trained myself to understand that one simply cannot eat unlimited amounts of *any* food (no, Virginia, you may *not* have four apples), my dieting attempts were frustrating and unsuccessful.

You think this hangup doesn't apply to you? Your geiger counter flutters madly whenever you even *approach* a salted peanut, and one must peer through a telescope to find the food on your plate. Perhaps, *just perhaps*, you eat little teensies, but *all the time*. If you merely have a speck of cheese and a tomato, but you have it at 11 A.M., again at 4, and once more before you go to bed (that's *in addition* to three meals), you're probably in weight trouble. Calories *do* add up.

The idea is that if you're *really* going to diet, lose pounds, change your eating habits forever and ever to *keep* them off, you must *develop a total consciousness* about what goes into your mouth. Remember this terrifying fact: If you were to add one 500-calorie dessert (a slice of apple pie à la mode, say) to whatever you now eat normally every day, you would gain fifty pounds in one year. And probably never understand *why!*

CHAPTER 4: ARE YOU A REFRIGERATOR RAPER?

Why are you overweight? Do you dislike shopping for clothes because the try-on mirror offers a painful confrontation with the Truth, feel unhappy standing naked in front of a new man, despise yourself during and after every binge, avoid walking across a room where people will stare at you, and yet, *with all that miserableness*, never lose weight?

Whether it's fifty pounds or seven, the problem is exactly the same. Oh, I know *your* history. (It's my own, after all.) You have tried nearly every diet—crash, slow, pills, Metrecal, whatever—when something *specific* motivated you! The coming of summer, a proposed trip to Hawaii, the appearance of a potential lover. You dropped a few pounds, or perhaps a tremendous amount; then for any one of forty-seven reasons (boredom, discouragement, overconfidence, loss of impetus), you gave up the diet and ate your way back to fat. Possibly you've gone through this cycle twice in one year! Here's my explanation: We Fat Souls have a craving for food that is far more powerful, aggressive, and demanding than our need for a good figure. We have been willing (unconsciously, of course) to pay the price of never really loving our looks, always feeling embarrassed and self-hating, because for us it's *more* crucial to eat.

If you, at this point, stamp your feet and hold your breath and turn blue and howl at me, "You're crazy! I want more than life itself to be thin and I just can't do it," I whisper back to you, "Nonsense." Look with scientific detachment and you'll just *have* to see that dropping pounds is very simple: You eat less, you get thin. Sickening from starvation is not a requirement; you eat lots of delicious things (I love shrimp cocktails even when I'm not dieting), and you get a sensational prize—a new, terrific body.

So why haven't you been able to do it? What in your head makes food so bloody important? Let's make a list, because there are multiple factors. How many sound familiar to you?

1. *Tension*. It's the biggest cause of neurotic eating. Thin Souls lose their appetites when nervous or anxious; *we* use food as a tranquilizer, tend to eat mountains to mollify those feelings. Next time you grab a fattening tidbit for no apparent reason, notice if there's stress and if the sensation lessens with the eating.

2. *To reward oneself*. Just like our mommies, we still think of food in terms of *treat*. Greta spent an entire three-day weekend painting her living room, an arduous job. When she finally finished on Sunday night, she phoned me and said, "I'm so proud of myself. Let's go have a banana split." I convinced her she'd be a lot prouder if she treated herself to a movie and a new suede belt.

3. *To punish oneself*. Have you just messed up your chances with a new man by being possessive too early in the game? Feeling like a flop? Want to feel even worse? Troop down to the neighborhood deli and buy a pastrami sandwich, a pound of potato salad, a bag of Fritos, two bottles of root beer, a pint of chocolate ripple ice cream. Go home and devour it all, every last bite, in one sitting. You'll *really* feel peachy afterward.

4. *Anger*. This emotion is harder to detect in oneself because the psychiatrists say that we frequently eat to hold *down* rage. (So it lurks unnoticed, right?) What you *can* see, though, is whether or not you attack food ferociously, cut and tear and chew with an overabundance of fervor. If so, you may well be a very angry person who's unwilling to deal with the *source* of rage.

5. *Depression, loneliness, need for solace, self-pity.* A lift undoubtedly results from a super meal. I can move from gloom to flawless contentment in a Chinese restaurant, picking away with chopsticks. But the comfort is obviously temporary if you're eating from misery (it truly ends the instant you *stop*), and if you indulge in a really heavy gorging session, you'll despise yourself midstream. (The link between your mental and biological states is being studied by a growing number of physicians and psychiatrists. Depression may even be causing you to metabolize certain foods more sluggishly than usual!) Depression and its corollaries are usual causes of binge eating— the irrational 11:30 P.M. dash to a store for candy, cookies, *and* ice cream, et al., ad nauseam. Binge eaters are frequently people who have normal food habits twenty-eight or so days a month, but go food-berserk when very sad.

6. *Lack of self-discipline.* Are you the type who had to stay up for seventy-two hours straight to write a college term paper assigned on the first day of class? Do you always mean to finish knitting that sweater that you started three years ago for your father? Do you never get around to answering letters? Are you invariably fifteen minutes late for work, two weeks late paying the rent? None of these characteristics has much to do with food, but they're symptoms of a personality that's not particularly self-disciplined or controlled—and since these qualities are (unfortunately) requisites for successful dieting, you may have weight problems because of them.

7. *Reaction to change.* Some people gain weight in direct relation to the stock market's decline (*or* rise). Others add pounds when moving to a new city or starting a new relationship. Food becomes a stabilizer, a *dependable.*

8. *Sexual frustration.* Did you ever wonder why the diet feels magnificent until *after* dinner, when everything goes haywire and you binge till sleep descends? Night eating is one of the commonest causes of diet doom, and doctors say it is almost *always* done alone, most often in secret. (Jean Nidetch, the Weight Watchers originator, used to hide

a chocolate cake in the clothes hamper and gobble it after her family went to sleep.) Night is when you're least active and sexual needs are most likely to surface. Their needs unmet, some people turn to food.

9. *Boredom, idleness.* When you're in the midst of schussing the Kandahar in St. Anton, it is highly improbable that your thoughts will focus on Wiener schnitzel and potato pancakes. On the other hand, staring at the wall for a whole evening waiting for *him* to call is an ideal scenario for refrigerator-rape.

10. *Orientation toward failure.* Some people (*you* aren't one of them, I know!) for exceedingly complex reasons need to lose at everything they attempt—jobs, love, sewing, diet. They make themselves fail, then say, "You see, I'm a failure..." and on and on in that good old vicious circle.

In most of the above cases, food replaces what one *really* craves—love, security, joy, freedom from stress. The key question: What are you *really* hungry for? Like alcoholics and drug addicts, the foodnik (you) absolutely must learn to deal with feelings and hangups in another way. Remember our motto: The answer to Life is not a strawberry malted!

When I was overweight, my shrink suggested that I had a fear of being thin, that I had something invested in remaining a dumpling. I screamed horrible insults at this man whom I'd been foolish enough to think was on my side. Full of hurt, I accused him of having *no* understanding of *me*, and once again sang the sad song of how tragic it was not to be able to wear a bikini, how grim to dread a medical checkup because the doctor always made me stand on the scale. But ... *after* I lost twenty pounds, I *knew* the psychiatrist was right. Lumpishness *had* been weirdly self-protective.

Example: If, while fat, I met a man at a party and he drifted away distractedly after talking to me for an hour, I assumed it was because I was pudgy, hence less lovely than eleven other girls in the room. Simple. Bearable. When the same kind of rejection occurred *after* I had become svelte, I was terrified. Devastated. What did it mean? What was *wrong* with me? What did he see in me that was evidently *worse* than being fat? Now of course this kind of thinking is illogical; some people are and always will be uninterested in you, for five hundred reasons. That's life. But I didn't learn that cruel bit of reality until I became thin. I never *had* to learn it before.

One way you might check to see if you want to stay fat (as unlikely as that seems) is to examine your daydreams and fantasies about life as a skinny lady. Do you think your whole existence will change if you lose ten pounds? Do you believe *he'll* marry you because of the new figure? If your ideas are so fancy, it's no wonder you may not want to risk their *not* coming true. Better to stay on the "if only" cloud. Better to stay plump.

Yet *another* characteristic about Fat Souls gives us trouble: absence of what psychiatrist Theodore Rubin (in his book *Forever Thin*, published by Bernard Geis Associates) calls the "enough-is-enough factor," the mechanism that says, "I'm full." A Fat Soul rarely feels stuffed; she stops eating when there's nothing left on her plate, on the table, in the refrigerator; or embarrassment at her gluttony *forces* her to stop. (Oh, the number of times I suddenly became painfully aware mid-dinner that I was putting away twice as much as my six-foot-tall date!)

To get physiological for a moment, the body machinery that causes the sensation of satiation is often called the "appestat," and it's located close to the base of the brain, near the pituitary gland. Doctors say that when it's off balance, you don't feel enough is enough. If you're not sure whether your appestat's in tip-top order, watch a friend, someone you consider a normal eater. Does he polish off everything on the table just because it's *there*, or does he pick and choose, eating only as much as he wants, leaving all sorts of goodnesses sitting in front of him? Do you?

Optimistic note: Dietary experts believe that the appestat can be reset like a thermostat and return to normal functioning after six weeks or so of nutritious, low-calorie dieting.

Finally, Fat Souls stay fat because of the Big Lie. Next to politicians, plumpies are the most outrageous liars in the world. All in the service of preserving our bulk, we invent incredibly complex ways to kid ourselves, muttering sentences like:

"I can lose ten pounds any time." (Translation: "I won't go on a diet now."

"My scale's broken."

"My mirror's crazy."

"I'm not fat, I'm sensual."

"Loose-fitting clothes are In."

"I'm too nervous to diet right now." (Translation: "I'll wait until my life is perfect, without any tension or problems.")

"The cleaner shrank my slacks."

"Five pounds doesn't show."

Such self-delusion can, and does, go on forever. Its purpose is to keep us blind—and fat. Alcoholics Anonymous, which has been so effective in helping problem drinkers, holds a ritual at the opening of each meeting: Every member stands up and introduces himself as "My name is Herman Feinschreiber and *I am an alcoholic*." That admission isn't supposed to shame him, but to make him *constantly* face and admit reality. Unless he acknowledges—in his guts, where he lives—that he is not merely a fellow who likes an occasional nip of the sauce but a full-bloomed alcoholic, he will never be successful at changing his drunken life-style. The A.A. technique is useful for overweights, too. (We've actually been called "foodaholics.") Until you can *really* confront the fact that it's not the scales, mirrors, or clothes-shrinkers falsely betraying you—but your body and head—you'll never get wonderfully, merrily, irrevocably *thin*.

Try adding your own self-deluding sentences to the examples I gave. (Mine used to be the postponement ploy: "I'll start dieting next Thursday, after I turn in the article that's giving me so much trouble." Next Thursday always came and went, as did my super intentions.)

Write your delusions here . . . *now!*

CHAPTER 5: WHY SHOULD YOU BE THIN?

My friend Penny, a weight battler for all her twenty-six years, dreams about finding a country where it's stylish to be soft and pudgy, where flesh is considered truly sexy, and where her fifteen surplus pounds will make her the most popular girl on the block. Certainly there have been magic lands like that (all those hefty dames in the Rubens paintings were the sex goddesses of seventeenth-century Flanders), but we don't happen to live in one. In the United States, where a vast segment of the population is overweight and the overwhelming national preoccupation is food, the most desirable goal, paradoxically, is to be as gaunt as possible and still remain alive! "A woman can never be too rich or too thin," said one top New York socialite in a newspaper interview, expressing what for many people are the primary values of life. Look at our models, movie queens, and fashions. Imagine trying to squeeze this season's St. Laurent show-stopper onto a Mama Cass form. Visualize most women in hot pants. Think about the clothes you've coveted lately, clearly designed for those with lean and hungry looks. The emphasis in our culture is on youth, thinness—and we can't *really* turn back the cultural clock to a time when fat was beautiful.

Yes, many women survive in our body-oriented society by comfortably *ignoring* its fashions and fetishes. They reside in loose clothes and flabby figures, and don't care. I envy them a bit, because so much of my own life has been a long fret over my shape. A large (of course!) portion of me would be overjoyed to prance in the same pair of blue jeans—even size sixteen—forever, eat anything I craved, and stop worrying about the whole monotonous issue! But on the other hand, if we choose to be in the mainstream of society, we must care about our physical—as well as our intellectual and emotional—selves. Liking and being pleased with yourself is crucial.

My cousin Joan, a divorcée in her early thirties, is a reporter for one of the largest weekly magazines in America. She claimed to be completely uninterested in clothing, exercise, diet, and all that frippery, considered it superficial, time-consuming, neurotic, and vain. I never argued with her, yet noticed that she not only withdrew from *those* shallow concerns but also from flirting with the attractive men in her office, from accepting invitations to appear on television talk shows, and from many, many social activities. Finally she came to realize (with a little help from her friends) that her *true* feeling wasn't boredom; it was fear of competing with women she considered more stylish and sexy. That's when she shed her extra baggage, visited the hairdresser, assaulted the sportswear department at Bloomingdale's—and began to feel slightly terrific about herself. Our *unequivocal promise:* You will like yourself so much better than you do now if you reach your ideal weight!

The most important motive for losing weight is the one I mention last, because realistically I know it's the least important to us vain creatures. Health. When somebody tells me my thighs are bulging from my bikini, I'm ready to sew up my mouth with rope; when I read that my life span is ten percent shorter if I'm that much overweight, I'm not motivated. (These responses apply to most other Fat Souls, obviously.) But let's be mature. Good health is our *most* vital concern, and being overweight or obese is *lethal.* Fact: "In the order named," says Dr. Benjamin A. Rosenberg, chief of the Obesity Clinic at Long Island College Hospital, in Brooklyn, New York, "coronary artery disease, biliary tract disease, cerebral hemorrhage, chronic nephritis, cirrhosis of the liver and diabetes, all show an increased mortality when associated with obesity. Coronary artery disease has a forty-two percent higher rate in the overweight; cerebral hemorrhage, fifty-nine percent; chronic nephritis, ninety-one percent." I don't know what some of those ailments are either, but let's try to focus on the scary implications of that statement. Read it again. . . . We, even in our twenties and thirties, are paving the highway to an early grave by stuffing our faces.

(A fascinating footnote: Although obese people die sooner from practically everything, they seem to be less susceptible than others to tuberculosis and suicide.)

If, for some perverse quirk of your own, the health statistics don't resound in your brain, try this: *Thin people enjoy sex more than fatties;* they have, according to researchers, more and bigger and better orgasms. I rest the case.

CHAPTER 6: PHYSIOLOGY AND NUTRITION 1A— A CRAM COURSE

Yes, *most* of our weight hangups are psychological. (We've talked about that, and the idea will come up often in this book.) But the *balance* of the problem (the *easiest* part to solve) is lack of information: not knowing the body functions in regard to food, what *specific* foods we can eat a lot of, what we can peck at *occasionally*, what foods to forget forever! We'll explore some of the common myths about dieting, detailing which are facts and which are fictions. Let's begin with physical *you*.

Think of your body as the engine of a car. (Don't you hate analogies like that? I do, too, but this is a good one!) The engine needs fuel to make it work, and food is the fuel. Simple so far? Now bear with me a bit—the analogy gets a little heavy—while I explain two necessary terms. A *calorie*—that dread word—is a unit of heat, contained in food. It is the fuel that's burned to provide the energy for the engine. When we say that an apple has 85 calories, we mean that it supplies your body with 85 calories of fuel energy. *Metabolism* refers to the *rate* of burning, or how many miles you get to the gallon. You may often hear a dieter say, "I have a low metabolism." If you *do* have a low metabolism (be sure you're not using this as an excuse, similar to the "It's my glands" ploy), you will indeed have more difficulty losing weight than someone who burns calories faster. *Most* people's metabolism functions normally.

Each individual requires a different number of calories to keep his engine running each day. The number you need depends on age, sex, and amount of activity. If you're a twenty-seven-year-old female secretary who spends most of her waking day sitting at the typewriter, followed by sitting in cabs, restaurants, movie theaters, and your boy friend's bed, you expend less energy (i.e., burn fewer calories) than the woman U.S. Tennis Open champion.

Weight gain means we've eaten *more* than we've burned in energy, and the excess is stored as fatty tissue. This doesn't mean, obviously, that you only burn calories by playing three sets of championship tennis. Metabolism goes on all the time, even while you rest or sleep. (Here's where that engine metaphor falls apart: Your *car* only burns fuel when it's actually *moving*.) Eating uses about 84 calories an hour for a 120-pound person; dressing and undressing, 108. (Writing, I've discovered, burns only 84, fewer than standing still!)

To lose weight, you simply (simply!) eat fewer calories than you need, so your body will be forced to draw its fuel supply from your surplus fat. In case you wonder why it seems to take so long to shed even a few pounds, let me explain the physiology: Every pound of fat on your body represents 3,500 stored extra calories. So, if you're twenty pounds overweight, you're holding *70,000 unneeded calories!* Now, to lose two pounds a week, which at this moment probably doesn't seem like very much, you'll have to use 7,000 calories of stored fatty tissue—or to put it another way, eliminate 1,000 calories a day from your diet. If you burn 2,200 calories a day, you'll have to cut out an extra 1,200 calories just to lose those two pounds a week.

The average American diet consists of fourteen percent protein, twenty-five to forty percent fat, the balance carbohydrates. Vitamins, minerals, water, and chemicals (food additives) are found to varying degrees in nearly every food, but do not contain calories. Very few foods are "pure" protein or carbohydrate, but it's important to know, for dietary purposes, whether you're eating something that has *essentially* protein or starch value.

WHAT'S A PROTEIN? Protein is the basic material of our cells. We cannot exist without it. It keeps our metabolism working normally, and is essential for cell repair, tissue-building, and growth. (One of the results of protein deficiency is stunted growth.) Proteins are digested more slowly than other elements, so they tend to retard hunger feelings. (Notice how much *earlier* in the day you crave lunch after eating a Danish pastry for breakfast as opposed to an egg.) In addition, they are bursting with all the key vitamins and minerals, except vitamin C.

Sources of protein are meat, poultry, eggs, fish, beans, nuts, some cereals, and cottage cheese. Lesser sources are milk, yogurt, and cheese. The problem with many protein foods, especially beef and pork, is that they are also liberally laced with fats.

SO, WHAT'S A FAT? There are two kinds of fats: hard fats (meat, eggs, milk products) and soft fats (found in most vegetable oils and seafood). Like carbohydrates, which we'll discuss next, fats provide much "fuel energy" quickly; and like proteins, they're digested at a slow rate, thereby satisfying you for long periods. (Fats actually slow down the emptying of the stomach.) They also contain the *most* calories per ounce, many more than proteins or carbohydrates. A pound of sugar, for instance, contains 1,000 calories; a pound of fat, 4,000.

One of the most vital discoveries in dietetics during the last decade has been the connection between hard (saturated) fats and disease, particularly heart disease and hardening of the arteries. These fats add blood cholesterol, a substance that clogs arteries and vessels, preventing free passage of blood. A balanced diet *ought* to supply enough of the special nutrients that *break up* cholesterol— but nowadays many of these nutrients are removed from food in processing. If you get a good supply of B vitamins (more about them in a minute)—*especially* in liver, yeast, wheat germ, kidney, brains, and egg yolk—you probably don't *have* a cholesterol problem. But we *would* all do better, whatever our ages, to *limit* consumption of saturated fats.

A CARBOHYDRATE? There are two kinds of carbohydrates: starches and sugar. They are the most abundant foods on earth, the major source of energy for most of the world's population, and forty-five to fifty percent of the American diet. Starch—that is, rice, corn, wheat, and flour products—is what dieters generally omit to shed weight. Fruits and vegetables contain carbohydrates, too, but in less-concentrated form because of their high water content. Sugar in these foods runs from a low of six percent (melon) to twenty percent (bananas). While sugar does provide instant energy (skiers frequently carry a chocolate bar in case they poop out on the way down the mountain), it doesn't *last* the way protein and fat energy do. On the other hand, the brain absolutely *requires* glucose (blood sugar) to function, so sugar (which your body makes into glucose) should never be totally omitted from your diet for a long time. (Exception: people with low blood sugar, a disease *completely unrelated* to the amount of sugar in the diet, should stay away from as much sugar as possible, and eat high-protein foods. Your doctor can give you a glucose test to determine low blood sugar.)

VITAMINS AND MINERALS You *need* minerals for healthy bones, blood, teeth, and metabolism. They don't provide calories, but *do* comprise four percent of your body weight. Key minerals: calcium (from dairy products and shellfish), iron (liver and other meats), and iodine (seafood and iodized salt).

Vitamins—"accessory food factors," the nutritionists term them—function to prevent disease. In parts of the planet where diets contain zero vegetables or milk products, vitamin deficiency is serious. Here, as more and more of us become one-a-day vitamin freaks, the debate rages about whether our diets are nutritionally adequate *without* vitamin *supplements*. It depends on which authority you choose to believe.

Here's the vitamin catalog: what they are, where to find them, what they do.

A—prevents dry skin, bad night vision, retarded growth of bones and teeth. Found in cream, egg yolk, liver, butter.

B-complex—for basic chemical processes in your cells. Deficiency causes beri-beri or pellagra. There are about fifteen B-complex vitamins, all working together as a group. The ones we know most about are:

Thiamine (B₁)—for brains, nerves, heart, and digestive tract. Found in whole wheat, peas, beans, bran, yeast.

Riboflavin (B₂)—for normal growth during childhood. Found in liver, milk, eggs, green vegetables.

Niacin—for resisting disease. Found in wheat germ, bran, fish, meat, yeast.

B_{12}—for blood cell development. Prevents pernicious anemia. Found in liver, milk, meats, fish.

C—for prevention and cure of colds, healing of wounds, maintenance of blood vessels and connective tissues, blood cell formation. Found in citrus fruits or juice, fresh raw fruits and vegetables.

D—for bone growth and proper absorption of calcium. Prevents rickets. Found in fatty fish (tuna, sardines, mackerel), eggs, butter, cheese.

E—for regulating metabolism within the cells, conserving oxygen. Some authorities believe this controversial vitamin will help prevent spontaneous abortions and heart disease. Found in wheat germ, unrefined, natural (not chemically processed) vegetable oils, whole-grain cereals, leafy vegetables.

K—needed for normal blood clotting. Most authorities believe an adequate diet, including milk and leafy green vegetables, eliminates the need for supplementary vitamin K.

If you want to know more about what vitamins and minerals can do for you (physically *and* emotionally), the following books are chock full of the details:

Food—The Yearbook of Agriculture, 1959. U.S.D.A. Washington, D. C., Superintendent of Documents, U.S. Government Printing Office, a complete yet clear text explaining what the essential food nutrients are, their value in a healthful diet, the role of calories, and how to select and prepare foods for greatest nutritional benefit, $3.25.

Davis, Adelle. *Let's Eat Right to Keep Fit.* Signet, $1.50.

Leverton, R. M. *Food Becomes You*. Iowa State University Press, $4.95.

Let's Talk About Food. American Medical Association, 535 North Dearborn Street, Chicago, Illinois, 60610, $2.00.

CHAPTER 7: CONFUSIONS AND MYTHS

This diet business is marbled with charlatanry the way a porterhouse steak is with fat. Quick answers, miracles, new crazes and theories appear daily. In addition, a great deal of ignorance persists among reputable dietitians and doctors whose lives are devoted to this area. We, the vulnerable, always looking for the magic key (I don't know about you, but I'm *still* waiting for the Enchilada and Chocolate Soufflé Diet!), are the victims. Each issue of every women's magazine sports a new, improved diet guaranteed to transform you. Biannually a new face with an M.D. attached marches onto a late-night talk show with his Big Solution. Ten years ago it was safflower oil. Last year, proteins and water. Next year? Rutabaga and Muenster cheese? Let's confront some of the myths and misconceptions.

MYTH #1. CALORIES DON'T COUNT— IT'S THE *KIND* OF CALORIES THAT MATTERS. False. This notion grew from a misinterpretation of SDA, the "specific dynamic action" of protein. SDA means that a hundred calories of meat are burned slightly faster than a hundred calories of doughnuts. Nutritionists have periodically escalated this minuscule difference—and it is truly tiny— to mean that the more protein you eat, the more weight you lose. (The theory: Increasing the protein in the diet stimulates metabolism, actually increasing the rate at which *all* food is being burned. Unfortunately, this just isn't so.)

In dieting, say most of today's mavens, calories are *all* that counts; and a calorie of spinach is *exactly the same* as a calorie of fudge. Remember, this means that if you're on a 1,200-calorie-a-day diet, it doesn't matter (in terms of losing weight) *how* you take those calories. Of course it *does* matter *nutritionally:* I would not like to see your insides, or your complexion, after four weeks of nothing but pecan pie or brown rice. But if, after strenuous successful dieting for a month, you crave a brownie with chocolate ice cream, you can go ahead *without going off your diet.* Understand that you will be consuming 450 calories, which have to come off your regular daily rate someplace. But the decision's yours: If you're willing to pay the price of, say, skipping dinner and going to bed hungry, then take the brownie and enjoy every morsel. That doesn't give you license to eat seven brownies and a quart of chocolate ice cream. (By the way, make it *ice milk!*) I know you binge eaters who think once you've been "bad," it doesn't matter what you shovel into your mouth afterward ... having lost control anyway, you may as well go totally to hell. Don't! Calories are everything! And a temporary relapse can be cured; total abandonment of discipline can't.

MYTH #2. STEAK IS GOOD; BREAD IS BAD. Wrong! You must forever blot from your brain this antiquated, erroneous, destructive dieting fallacy. Years ago, when I used to diet badly, I assumed the best way was living on salad and steak ... huge portions of meat, usually with fat included. What I eliminated were desserts, bread, and potatoes. The "classic" diet, no? Well, let's examine that assumption, calorie for calorie (the only thing that counts, remember).

CALORIC CONTENT OF BEEF (3½-ounce portion)

	Protein	Fat	Total
Porterhouse steak	108	134	242
Standing rib roast	95	190	285
Ground chuck	109	154	263

Not only are those calorie counts surprisingly high, but did you ever *just* eat three and a half ounces of steak? That's about three slices! To estimate an average portion, double the calorie counts above. The reason for this exorbitant caloric price is the amount of fat; all those meats have more fat than protein. Limiting your intake of beef (also lamb and pork) and substituting fish, chicken, and veal will make you a champion pound-loser.

CALORIC CONTENT OF BEEF ALTERNATIVES
($3\frac{1}{2}$-ounce portion)

	Protein	Fat	Total
Roast chicken	156	27	183
Baked bluefish	130	29	159
Veal cutlet	163	39	202

Bread is another maligned food: There is no reason for you to *cancel* it from your life. *It's not all that fattening.* A slice of white bread has 65 calories, whole wheat 55. Muffins, rolls, bagels, are more, but the real villains are those innocent-looking crackers! Dieters often prepare a virtuous salad for lunch, and since they won't eat the dreaded monster, bread, they'll nibble on ten Saltines instead, feeling very sacrificial and consuming *150* calories. Over recent years I've *conditioned* myself to order a sandwich for lunch—cheese, white-meat turkey, or roast beef—and then to discard the top slice of bread. Order open-faced sandwiches wherever you can. The biggest danger in bread is the butter or mayonnaise you glop all over it!

MYTH #3. THE MYSTICAL PROPERTIES OF GRAPEFRUIT . . . AND OTHER TALL TALES. Several years ago everyone I knew went on a regimen under which every meal began with half a grapefruit. You were not, under penalty of death, to omit the grapefruit. The idea was not just that this food was nutritious, but that it had a "special agent" to act in some mysterious metabolic way on the meal that followed, causing massive loss of weight. None of that magic would happen, one was assured, without the grapefruit.

Then there was the diet, popularized just recently by one of the women's magazines, that claimed you must drink a glass of dry white wine with every meal (breakfast?) because wine aids in absorption of other foods.

My friend Arnold's occult combination is oranges and lamb chops, which he insists is a hot tip for hurry-up svelteness.

Grapefruit is a wonderful, adorable food. I would hate to contemplate life without it. But it has *no* mystical talent for turning fat into thin, exerting some special power over absorption, metabolism, digestion, or the like. The same for white wine. Or *anything*. These superstitions develop because we believe everything we *want* to believe—looking for quick, glib answers. Fatties particularly want an *easy* solution *desperately* because dieting is *hard* work. Arnold lost eighteen pounds in a month on nothing but oranges and lamb chops because (1) he's a hyperenergetic young man who undoubtedly burns 500 calories a minute, and (2) because he got so sick of oranges and lamb chops, he practically stopped eating altogether.

MYTH #4. SALT. (A) USE IT FREELY. (B) DON'T USE IT AT ALL. The truth about salt is that we only require one gram a day, or a fifth of a teaspoon, to keep a water balance in our bodies. (Salt makes the tissue hold water.) Most Americans consume about ten to twenty times that, meaning we may be retaining up to four extra pints of water. The reason we generally drop a good many pounds during the first few days of dieting is that we are losing that excess liquid through the natural diminution of salt intake as we consume less food.

Water losses are tricky things and should never be mistaken for a fat exodus. If you sit in a steam box, you'll drop a few pounds of water; take a diuretic pill, you again lose water. Stop eating salt, the same weight loss occurs. But these are all temporary drops, and you shouldn't concentrate on or fret over them. Salt food lightly; you'll lose excess water through normal dieting. If, after several weeks, you reach a plateau where you're not losing, try eliminating *all* additional salt for a while. Your body may again, in its readjustment, be clutching onto water in its tissues.

MYTH #5. LOSING WEIGHT MAKES YOUR SKIN SAG. Women suffer tremendous fear that after all the labor of dieting they will emerge thin, yes—but with revolting, baggy, loose skin. Fad-diet proclaimers take advantage of that myth by statements like "The new miraculous beer-and-broccoli regimen leaves skin firm and tight." In my own experience, my skin looked much better as I became thin, because there was so much less of it! Doctors say that the flesh is young and resilient for those under forty; and elasticity remains after weight loss, so the skin automatically contracts and shrinks. Stop worrying—and above all, stop using this excuse not to diet.

MYTH #6. DIETETIC FOODS ARE BEAUTIFUL. Well, some of them are (I thank the stars for dietetic Jell-O, strawberry jam, and Cool Whip), but many are shockingly deceptive—either only slightly fewer calories than their nondietetic counterparts, or sometimes even more. Yes, *more!* In *The All-in-One Diet Annual* (by Peter Wyden and Lois Libien, Bantam Books), the authors compare regular and dietetic cookies, and here's the bad news:

COOKIES: CALORIES PER OUNCE

	Regular	Dietetic
Coconut cookie	140	154
Chocolate-chip cookie	134	100–136
Chocolate and vanilla sandwich	140	103–133

The same is true of candy: One ounce of regular chocolate-covered raisins has 120 calories; the dietetic, 133.

You must be very cautious and alert with dietetic foods. Read labels carefully. A tablespoon of Peter Pan diet peanut butter has 100 calories; regular also has 100. A pint of ice cream with the word "dietetic" emblazoned all over it may lure you into thinking it's safe, but beware: A third of a pint of vanilla diet ice cream contains 175 calories, only 20 fewer than nondietetic, but 40 *more* than *any flavor* of ice milk. (Besides, diet ice cream tastes awful, and many dietetic foods contain chemical additives that can endanger your health more than the sugar they replace!)

The following chart shows the spectrum of differences between regular and dietetic versions of the same foods—from caloric variances that are enormous, to cases where the calories saved are negligible, to instances where dietetic versions are actually *more* fattening.

	Quantity	Calories Regular	Calories Dietetic
Salad dressing (Italian)	1 tablespoon	85	8
Chocolate syrup	1 tablespoon	50	14
Canned apricots	$\frac{1}{2}$ cup	98	56
Cream of mushroom soup	4 ounces	120	69
Canned green beans	$\frac{1}{2}$ cup	13	17
Vegetable juice	4 ounces	22	24
Chocolate bar	1 ounce	152	160

Never assume anything!

CHAPTER 8: QUACKS AND CRAZIES

Dancing cheek-to-cheek with the myths and ignorances about fatness are the people who take advantage—frauds, nuts, snake-oil salesmen, magicians—who claim to have a mystical super-solution to the dilemma of overweight. I have tried—or know someone who has tried—every possible fast trick for losing weight, and I am here to tell you it is all hot-airsville. One little story will show how susceptible Fat Souls are to *anything* that promises thinness without work, weight loss without dieting:

When I was sixteen, owner of a figure without indentations from shoulders to knees, my two best girl friends and I found a diet "expert" . . . the ex-wife of a local dentist. When he ran off with his X-ray technician, Mrs. Dentist turned the offices into a reducing salon. I paid her ten dollars an hour. She made me lie naked on a surgical table; about thirty wires were attached at one end to a giant, formidable machine, at the other end taped to my skin. Each treatment placed the wires on a section of my body that Mrs. Dentist thought needed slimming (admittedly, she *did* have an unlimited choice), one week the calves, next week the thighs. . . . Then she'd turn on the machine and—believe it or not—every ten seconds I got a horrendous electric shock and a fierce contraction of skin. She stood by the machine like some horror-movie lunatic, turning up the current each time I adjusted to the previous shock. The electric current was supposed to cause *permanent* muscle contractions, so I'd lose endless inches. Marilyn and Linda and I were electrocuted $150-worth each (every cent I had saved) until our mothers found out (and we realized that our waists became teeny for two hours, then spread back to normal). I tell you this grotesque, absurd tale because Fat Souls expose ourselves to fakery like this—and worse—*every* day.

The American Medical Association says that food quackery is the most profitable form of charlatanry in the United States. It claims that five-hundred million dollars a year is spent by the public on reducing pills, cure-alls, slenderizing machines, food supplements, massages.

The "fat-doctors" are the arch villains, in my opinion. (Also the richest of the fakers. Most make more than a hundred thousand dollars a year.) Here's how they work (I tried this, too!): Dr. Fat's office is like a bakery. You take a number and wait your turn. The other "customers," about forty of them the day I was there, run the gamut in age and body type. When finally it's time for your medical examination, the doctor weighs you, takes blood pressure, and asks if you've ever had heart trouble. Period. He then gives you a mimeographed diet and a month's supply of pills—green, yellow, brown, white—with detailed instructions about which and how many to take when. ("Two green after lunch, a brown and a white at 4 P.M., one yellow before bed," and so on.) Chemical analysis proves the pills to be amphetamines for appetite depression, diuretics to get rid of water (and to show an immediate loss on the scale), and tranquilizers to *counteract* irritability from the amphetamines.

Why do I knock this method? Number one, you've not been given a *real* physical examination. What if you're a diabetic, or have some kidney problems? Indiscriminate use of pills can do devastating damage to your body. These quacks know it, and don't care.

Secondly, I'm utterly against diet pills even for the perfectly healthy. I have lost literally hundreds of pounds with pills over the years, and would never use medicines again. (When I finally lost my Big Twenty, no pill passed my lips the entire time.) Benzedrine and dexedrine, the two classic appetite depressants, produce—when taken in big enough doses—"speed freaks," and even in dieters' quantities, make for extreme jumpiness, heart palpitations, inability to sleep, and depression. (At a drug conference recently, experts stated that more speed freaks are little ladies on reducing diets than hippies in the drug culture.)

Like the way it sounds so far? "Well," you're probably saying to yourself, "I'll pay that price because the little 'dolls' will kill my otherwise overpowering hunger and I'll get skinny." Indeed appetite depressants do destroy one's appetite to the point where, for the first week, you'll have to force yourself to swallow *anything*. (What a new sensation *that* is!) Unfortunately, the effect doesn't last because, as with any addictive drug (yes, you can easily become a diet-pill junkie), you develop increased tolerance and must take ever larger doses to get the same effect. Meanwhile, you are sleeping badly, losing friends due to your moods and jumpiness, and above all, not changing your eating *patterns*. You can't stay on pills forever, and when you stop, what happens? I'll tell you: You'll gain back every ounce. Honest!

The psychological reasons for shunning the valley of the dolls should be even more convincing. Probably you've always felt a slave to food, to crazy, uncontrollable cravings. Now you'll be a slave to the little pill, still feeling powerless over your life and believing you can't meet the dietary challenge without a crutch. What you must do is build your self-esteem, the feeling that your body is your responsibility, with you in charge. If you lose excess weight under your own power (and you *will*), you'll feel really proud of conquering the challenge, thrilled with your own strength and capacity for control. You'll never feel again, "I can't do it," because you'll have done it. *Yourself.*

Stay away from reducing salons. Also preying on our gullibility, they sell the fantasy "effortless exercise," plus machines that ostensibly do the work (you just sit there and the contraption exercises!) for hundreds of dollars. People sign up for long-term, expensive "courses" and massage. Let's spell it out right away: *Massage does not get rid of fat.* Sorry, sisters. Nor does it (as these operations claim) increase muscle, firm the body, or change the metabolism. It just feels nice. That's all.

The most terrifying scandal I've come across was the diet pill that guaranteed you could eat anything you wanted and still lose mountains. The pills actually worked beautifully . . . they contained tapeworm eggs.

Girdles that supposedly remove inches while you wear them, sofas that jiggle your fat while you sit, belts with battery motors that contract waist muscles —worn under clothes and costing a mere $69.95—all make money for their sponsors, but there's not a grain of scientific logic in any of them.

HOW YOU CAN GET THIN

All the previous chapters about the prompt-ings that make you fat and the benefits of being thin—plus the quickie physiology course—are necessary before you start dieting. You must understand why you stay fat before you try to get thin. (That's basic Psychology 1A, right?) But those insights clearly aren't enough impetus to drop un-needed, undesirable poundage and to drop it *forever*.

Unfortunately, I can't convince you to lose weight. Eating is too much fun, too seductive, and has been too potent a force in your life for a mere book (however bril-liant and powerful and witty!) to make you psychologically ready to get thin. That's your job alone. If you have been reading along happily, waiting for me to *motivate* you magically, you'll be disappointed. You must want thinness yourself, from deep inside.

What that motivation takes is a brutally honest acknowledgment that you are overweight. Stop blaming the faulty scale, Sam the Tailor, or whomever. Stop pretending you eat like a pigeon and couldn't lose anyhow. Stop saying you've been dressing in the wrong styles. Stop telling yourself you're eight pounds overweight when the true figure is twenty-eight. *Stop deceiving yourself about yourself.*

Stand nude in front of your full-length mirror and really confront that body. Pinch the thighs. Hold on to the tummy flesh. Jiggle your arms and buttocks to see how much is loose and flabby. Turn sideways now. How about the pot belly, the outsized fanny? Is this truth too painful to bear? Is it enough to make you shatter the mirror into a thousand pieces? Good! You're on the way.

You must also feel an absolute inability to tolerate the situation of being plump for another day. *You cannot stand it any more.* None of this I'll-begin-a-week-from-Tuesday nonsense. Uttering that phrase undoubtedly means you're not ready to shed your blubber, you still need it to hide behind.

Ready? Really ready? O.K., let's begin tomorrow morning. As for tonight—go out and gorge yourself! That's right, go to a supermarket and buy every single item you want to eat tonight, no matter how fattening. Doughnuts, ice cream, spaghetti, spareribs —anything. Or get your man to take you to your favorite restaurant, and eat until they have to carry you out. Do it without guilt or remorse. Send off the old you in style. For tomorrow you start a *new* adventure with food . . . one that will last for the rest of your life.

First step: See your friendly family doctor. Not the shady fat-doctor with the pills, but the nice white-haired general practitioner with the stethoscope. Tell him you're embarking on a full-fledged diet. He'll begin by weighing you on his flawless scale. (Don't forget—that scale *is* calibrated to perfection, even though it may register five pounds more than you *think* it should.) Have a complete external-internal checkup with electrocardiogram, chest X-ray, and basal metabolism test.

Now, you're undoubtedly in sparkling health, but you may have some special quirks—allergies, high blood pressure, diabetes—which will need consideration when you plan the Perfect Diet. If you get weird splotches from clams, better to know it now than later. You may need an especially low-salt diet (easy to arrange), or your doctor may want you to stop taking birth control pills if you're an extreme water retainer. If you're an unfortunate with constipation trouble, you need a diet abundant with roughage.

Get the doctor's ideas about vitamins. My own believes that any diet of under 1,500 calories a day requires a multiple vitamin tablet in the morning; others say no.

Ask your doctor to figure out, to the best of his ability, how many calories you burn a day. A general rule (general rules have many exceptions, however) for young women between twenty and forty is to multiply your desired weight by 15 if you're sedentary (that is, you spend more than six hours a day sitting, less than one hour moving strenuously), or by 20 if you're vigorous (that probably applies to none of us—it means walking or exercising ten hours a day, or your entire work day spent in physical labor!) The result is the number of calories you can consume each day without either gaining or losing weight. My ideal weight is 135 pounds, and my workaday life keeps me slumped at a typewriter, inertia relieved only by the periodic exercise of changing the ribbon; so I probably burn in the neighborhood of 2,025 calories a day. Ask your doctor what he thinks about this method of computing the calories you need.

Pick your doctor's brain about a workable diet. You may find he's too conservative for your needs (some of them are thrilled pink if you lose half a pound a week), but listen to his notions anyway. Remember, he sees Fat Souls about five times a day, and may just know something that you or I don't. Confide in him your particular difficulties, cravings, needs. My doctor once pointed out to me that the 4:15 fatigue I feel every day is metabolic, explaining my surging lust for chocolate. (My blood-sugar level is low at that time of day.) A *diet* root beer not only keeps me from collapsing into an hour's ill-afforded nap, but quiets my urge for sweets. You probably have a few similar idiosyncracies.

If you think you need regular visits to your doctor for motivation—it's no shame—plan to see him once a week just to get weighed. Every visit costs you money, so you're less likely to cheat from week to week. (The same theory explains why psychoanalysts *should* be expensive.) Also, we *all* need support, a firm-but-loving scold, and some *applause.* He can help you over those plateaus when you're just not losing, or explain why that Chinese-dinner splurge last week may have meant the difference between a two-pound and a one-pound loss. Or, bless him, he'll shriek with joy when you've had a spectacular week—which you *will!*

Second step: Determine what *you* want to weigh. Most diet manuals tend to treat everybody alike. They chart your ideal weight depending on height, age, and bone structure—then give you *their* diet to follow. This is not the proper procedure. It's much too general to be effective.

To begin with, forget the charts—whether you see them in books or on the scale in the ladies' room of your neighborhood movie palace. Be realistic about what *you* want to weigh. No Audrey Hepburn fantasies, however. Have you ever been a weight that was perfect for you? What was it? My 5' 7" frame looks best at 133 to 136. (At least *I* think it looks best, which is what counts.) My friend Jeannette is my height but can't stand how she feels or looks when she tops 116 on the scale. She's smaller-boned than I, smaller-breasted and -fannied, and looks simply terrific twenty pounds thinner than I am at *my* perfect weight —although we're the same height!

So, decide on your ultimate goal—and remember it. If you get discouraged six pounds away from bull's-eye, avoid thinking: "Oh, I look all right at *this* weight. I'll just stay here." Lose what you originally said you wanted to lose—don't stop short. (What is more likely to happen is that when you reach the goal, you'll feel so confidently perky you'll want to try losing a few *more* pounds, just to see how you look without *them*. Go ahead. If you're too lean— well, we *know* you're an expert at putting on weight fast!)

Third step: Make a Diet Profile of yourself (to help you find that Perfect Diet we've talked about). What you must do right here is painstakingly examine *your* eating patterns, *your* tastes, *your* needs. This diet is going to be your excursion, and must be utterly tailored to pamper your desires and requirements.

Kay, for instance, has two children and a pantry brimming over with peanut butter and Oreo cookies. She has found through experience that with all those nibbles around she must put herself on a very rigid protein-and-vegetable regime—*nothing* else—or she cheats with a leftover cracker here, an uneaten half-sandwich there. Another dieter, Jack, would rather burst than let a mouthful of seafood pass his lips, so *his* diet must accommodate that eccentricity. Yours will be geared to *you*.

As a start toward Knowing Thyself, answer these basic questions:

1. Could you happily live on steak alone?

2. Would you perish without an apple a day?

3. Are you someone who can't swallow a morsel before noon?

4. Are you a night eater (consuming half your daily calories *after* 7 P.M.)?

5. Are you the feast-or-famine, all-or-nothing type?

6. Will you get the screaming meemies without a Scotch-and-soda after work?

7. Do you adore the computations of counting and apportioning calories?

8. How do you honestly feel about vegetables?

9. Does your skin break out from fish? Strawberries? Anything?

10. Do you require variety? Or does a big choice of foods tempt you too distractingly?

Really *think* about these questions. Add as many of your own as you can possibly dream up. If you're still uncertain of your needs, you'll probably have to experiment with several different diets before you find one that seems to work. Don't be ashamed if you spend a couple of weeks trying several, switching diets every four days or so. As long as you're cutting down your calories, you'll be losing weight no matter *how* much experimentation you do.

Need it be said that finding the right diet for you, one that will be most fun, satisfying, and livable, least depriving and painful, will *never* be titled the Mashed Potatoes and Gravy Diet? Don't be naïve and say, "But you told me to consider my needs, and I *need* a prune Danish for breakfast." You *know* what I mean.

Having asked and answered the basic diet questions and made up a Diet Profile for yourself, you're ready to find the Perfect Diet. If, for example, you answered a loud "Yes" to Question 1—if you are a meat freak—you'll probably want to try the Stillman Diet or Dr. Atkins's *Cosmopolitan* or *Vogue* diets, all of which permit unlimited quantities of meat. If you're a chronic night nibbler, you might undergo the Weight Watchers' regimen, where you can save your three alloted pieces of fruit and two glasses of milk for those witching hours. Are you the feast-or-famine gal? Maybe you'd find it easiest to stick to the Eating Man's Diet (900 calories one day, 2,500 the next).

The super-successful diets are spelled out for you to make your selection from in the next chapter.

CHAPTER 10: THE SUPER-SUCCESSFUL DIETS

The truest cliché that I know about dieting is that *any low-calorie* diet will work, provided you stick to it. Whether it will wreck your health and welfare is another matter. Well, we, of course, are *supremely* concerned about being *healthy,* so no program will be considered here (neither should *you* consider one) that could jeopardize your well-being. But let's think about some of the styles available to you:

SLOW OR SPEEDY? Is it better to get the pounds all off quickly, or a teeny bit at a time? Each theory has its pros and cons—again, your choice depends on personal needs. What can be said for going on a crash diet that knocks pounds off in a flash is that you get *instant* rewards and gratification. If you have a good bit of weight to banish, the thought of parting with a mere one or one half pound each week may be too discouraging to bear, may turn you off before you *start*. In that case, it could be weeks before you even spy a tiny change in your dimensions. Or perhaps you're only five or so pounds above normal: Your instinct might be to starve yourself just above survival level for a week, and hustle it all off *fast*. On the con side of the crash ledger is this fact: Taking it off—however you do it—is the easiest part. *Keeping* thin is the rub. On a long-term regimen you accomplish two goals for lifetime thinness: (1) You learn all about foods and dieting, and (2) you have a chance to really change those naughty eating habits you've acquired over the years. Neither of those results happens with crash dieting. You lose your five or twenty-five pounds *zap!*—then you go right back to French fries for lunch, Hollandaise sauce on your broccoli. You haven't learned or changed an iota, except for those pounds—which we know can be retrieved instantaneously. The statistics about crash dieting for loss of large amounts are disastrous: Ninety-nine percent of the people who crash to normal weight regain every pound within two years. Many—from a masochistic sense of failure, I suppose—even put on more than they began with.

I think the answer to this fast/slow dilemma is to start with a bang, for a week or so, then relax into a respectable, intelligent, two-pounds-a-week diet for however long it takes you to reach the desired weight. My brother lost forty pounds or so (which he's kept off) by fasting for one week, under a doctor's care (vitamin shots every day), during which he lost sixteen pounds, then going onto a regular high-protein diet for several months. That system solved a multitude of problems, in that he was exhilarated after the first week, totally inspired to greater heights of accomplishment. Since then, too, his eating patterns have changed almost completely.

TO COUNT OR NOT TO COUNT CALORIES?
We know that calories do indeed count; that, alas, they are the only things that *do*. The question is, what are the benefits of carrying around in your head a little computer that registers, "This has 42 calories. This has 212"? Well, you *will* know precisely what you are eating. No cookie morsels, dabs of jelly added to toast, or ten pretzels at the bar can be indulged in without that calorie computer telling you what you're doing. (Of course, calorie counters can deceive themselves, too—it's just a bit harder.) Whether you're on a 1,200-a-day or 900-a-day diet, you'll be your own little adding machine (especially if you're dutifully writing everything down in your little diet diary) and will be less likely to cheat.

On the other hand, I find calorie-counts supremely *boring*. Not only is the tallying cumbersome and compulsive ("Let's see, does six ounces of halibut have more than six ounces of chicken leg?"), but it makes you focus on food in a joyless way. Also, there's a built-in trap: People tend to give up fruit or milk in order to justify eating a bagel with butter. Now, I'm not totally opposed to cheating nutritionally *once in a very great while*—that is, if you've been good as a gold nugget for several weeks, then decide to forego your normal dinner for a bag of potato chips. But Fat Souls are not famous for our ability to make wise judgments about food, so I fear the potato-chip syndrome might start happening three times a week, perhaps followed by the "I'll skip lunch and dinner and just have a pint of butter pecan ice cream" disease.

Calorie counters, for some odd reason, never keep their tallies to themselves, but need to involve everybody they know (probably because the task is so dull they need company). Haven't you ever sat at lunch with one, forced to listed ad nauseam to "The bread sticks have 114, and the Scotch has 85, and there are 32 in the boiled beets." The answer is, I suppose, that if you like the mathematics, promise not to bore your eating companions to death, and beware of the substitution traps, calorie counting probably will work for you.

OCCASIONAL FASTING. A model I know, gaunt beyond belief but naturally obsessed with her figure, fasts every Monday and Tuesday. She wakes up to a selection of vitamin supplements prescribed by her family doctor, of course, then consumes nothing but black coffee, tea, bouillon, or diet sodas. Mystics say periodic fasting restores harmony to the soul. I would say this: Having done it a few times myself (usually after a gorging Thanksgiving or just pre–Virgin Islands), I can testify that the first twelve hours are hell; I felt wildly hungry and a bit headachey. Then, as everyone predicts, you do indeed lose your appetite totally and feel rather tranquil. Your sleep improves, too. I would not suggest mountain climbing during a two-day fast. I would also advise against fasting more than *very* occasionally, or continuing if you feel the slightest bit ill. And don't forget the *vitamins!* They're essential when fasting.

SKIPPING MEALS. I promise I won't lecture you about breakfast—well, not too much. By all means eliminate lunch from your life if you'd rather shop at midday, or stay in the office and write a letter; and give up dinner if you're simply not hungry or want to catch a triple-feature flick instead. But breakfast (the only meal that people tend to skip, ironically) gets the engine going for the day—to use that old analogy again—and you won't aid your diet at all by skipping it. Without breakfast, the processes that act to burn up calories are sluggish, don't function at full speed. *Force* yourself to eat breakfast if you must (you'll get into the habit quickly, though), and make sure it contains some protein, not just juice and coffee. You see, I'm lecturing you about breakfast. . . .

SIX MEALS A DAY. Many nutritionists back the notion that snacking six times a day is better dieting technique than the usual three meals. Again, what's your own personal style? Have you always been a "nosher," unable to pass the refrigerator without halting for a fleeting but fulfilling visit? Just remember, nibbling between all three meals means you've got to cut down the basic three, right?

STILLMAN DIET. On this exceedingly popular, simple, and successful diet you can only eat five things, *nothing else:* lean meat, fish, chicken or turkey, cottage cheese, and boiled or poached eggs (no frying, all fat removed from foods, but in any quantities you want). You may also have the ubiquitous black coffee, tea, diet soda, but you must *without fail* drink eight glasses of water a day. A lot of people I know have lost a ton of weight on this diet. One advantage: You don't have to count calories. Also, you can always find a steak or broiled sole in any restaurant you're taken to. What seems to happen after a week or so is that the monotony makes you stay on but hardly eat at all. I personally loathe this diet because after two days I would kill for an orange. Many friends find the rigidity effective for their particular psyches. Consult *The Doctor's Quick Weight Loss Diet* by Dr. Irwin Stillman and Samm Sinclair Baker (Dell paperback, $1.25) for particulars.

LIQUID FORMULAS. With the flavored dietetic canned drinks that you get in the supermarket—Metrecal, Carnation Slender, and the like—you drink one can (approximately 225 calories each) four times a day. Nothing else. Rigid and easy: You don't have to worry about temptations or snitching a little more than you should. In addition, the liquids do fill you up, and can be carried in pocketbook or kept in desk drawer. I've never known anyone who could stick with a liquid diet for more than a couple of days, but it's probably an easy and effective way to *begin* dieting.

COSMOPOLITAN YES YES! NO NO! TEN-DAY DE-HUNGRIFICATION DIET. Have you ever starved yourself almost to *extinction,* counting every ignoble calorieless day-after-day-after-day, only to fling up your hands (in the direction of the refrigerator) in a final, humiliating tidal wave of hunger? Well, at last someone understands, and hunger may have given you your last nightmare, thanks to the findings of Dr. Robert C. Atkins, leading New York bariatrician (M.D. who specializes in obesity), who says, "Hunger is an unnecessary hardship. Dieting should *always* be associated with a feeling of well-being . . . being full. The person who begs off a diet because she doesn't feel well has never been exposed to the *correct* diet!" That's why Dr. Atkins developed his Carbohydrate Deprivation Diet—the De-Hungrification Diet—so that only the *carbohydrates* would feel deprived.

In fact, Dr. Atkins's low-carbohydrate/high-protein-and-fat-diet (not a new concept, though considerably refined) carries double its weight: The fewer carbohydrates you consume, the faster and more easily you lose weight; at the same time, your hunger lessens without gnawing awareness. Sound like fantasy? According to Dr. Atkins and several thousand lightweight followers, it is fact. "Carbohydrate foods," Dr. Atkins explains, "such as cookies, potatoes, and other sugars and starches tend to *stimulate* the appetite, make you hungry for more, more, *more.* Proteins and fats—such as meats, eggs, cheese, butter—*satiate* the cravings. When carbohydrates are taken out of the diet, the appetite is remarkably diminished, and the individual automatically restricts her intake of other foods because of a marked loss of appetite."

If the doctor's patients are any indication, this theory *works*. Part of the reason is, as Dr. Atkins explains, that "Fat is stored on the body as reserve fuel as long as carbohydrates are taken in. But if you stop feeding your body carbohydrates, that stored fat must be used as fuel instead. The fate of the fats you eat while *on* the low-carbohydrate diet has never been traced, although two British doctors discovered a fat-mobilizing hormone that the body makes when no carbohydrates are eaten, and that allows stored fat that contains calories to be *sneaked out* of the body. It is absolutely incorrect that the body *needs* carbohydrates . . . unless it has used up *all* of its fat."

The doctor advocates taking megadoses of vitamins while dieting (E, C, and a B-complex) and cutting out any other nonessential medication. He also suggests you first try *any* low-calorie diet for ten days, *then* ten days of his diet, so you can compare results. But he *does* insist on strict adherence once you are *on* the Atkins diet, and during that time he is a stern taskmaster. "One slice of bread," he emphasizes, "has impact—twenty grams of carbohydrates can have a significant effect. Even a tablespoon of potato salad will throw the balance off." And, though he says inches disappear easily with his diet (most people lose ten pounds or more in ten days), he recommends some exercise daily.

"Most dieters," he says, "have a lifelong pattern of flagging motivation, and no diet, not even mine, will work without some will power. A patient has to give it an absolutely fair, no-cheat trial to see if the alleged benefits pertain to her as an individual. There *should* be freedom from hunger, satiety, an upsurge of energy and improvement of mental alertness, plus easier, more rapid weight loss than on any other diet. But if a patient does not *strictly* adhere to the diet, she ends up on only a low*ish*-carbohydrate diet with such symptoms as fatigue, depression, and irritability; she may then come to the conclusion that she doesn't feel well because of the diet." Remember, the purpose of this diet is to induce the dieter to use up her stored fat as fuel, by avoiding the ready fuel—carbohydrates. If a dieter cheats and eats potato chips, she's not getting enough carbohydrates to burn off as fuel, but just enough to prevent her burning her *fat* off as fuel. No wonder she feels terrible! Dr. Atkins goes on, "I believe the side effects of an improper low*ish*-carbohydrate diet are the key to most dieters' psychiatric (mental) problems. That's why I'm *into* this ultra-low carbohydrate diet, because I believe *every* dieter is entitled to experience the feeling of well-being."

Now let's get on to the *diet*. Here's our Yes Yes! No No! ten-day plan to melt off ten pounds *without* leaving you hungry . . . but only if you don't *cheat!* Ready? Remember:

1. This is a carbohydrate-deprivation test to be tried for ten days *only* in order to see how your body reacts to a diet virtually free of starches and sugars so that your own stored fat will be used as a source of energy.

2. The diet will be *negated* if you add so much as a single pretzel stick or other item not listed below.

3. Again, this is *not* a permanent diet but rather to see if you do better on a low-carbohydrate diet than a low-calorie one.

Breakfast

Two eggs prepared any style, including fried in butter (if you're cooking an omelet, make it without milk)

Ham, bacon, cheese (see cheese list), or smoked fish, if desired

Coffee, tea, or bouillon; lemon in tea; heavy cream in coffee

Lunch

100-percent-beef hamburger, *or*

Tongue, corned beef, pastrami, *or*

Fish, shellfish, canned tuna, canned salmon, or smoked fish as main dish

Small green salad with Italian dressing made of oil, vinegar, and all spices except sugar; add anchovies or grated cheese for extra flavor. Salad greens: romaine, endive, escarole, lettuce, celery, cucumbers, radishes and peppers *or* one small pickle (sour or dill) as a substitute for the salad

Coffee, tea, bouillon, sugar-free soda

Dinner

Seafood cocktail (use mayonnaise, not cocktail sauce), *or*

Smoked fish

A main dish of meat, fish, or chicken broiled (in butter, if you like)

Small green salad with Italian dressing (see lunch)

Coffee, tea, bouillon, club soda, sugar-free soda

Coffee Breaks and Snacks

Fried pork rinds

Cucumber spears

Beef broth, club soda

D-Zerta, Jell-O, or unflavored Knox gelatin you flavor yourself with extracts

One or two cold shrimp without sauce

Small chunk of cheese

Trident or Bazooka Sugarless Bubble Gum (only three sticks a day)

Yes Yes! Foods (amounts per day)

Meats, eggs, fish, seafood, chicken: as much as you like of any not on No No! list.

Salad greens: two cupfuls

Cheeses: three ounces of Swiss, Cheddar, Brie, Camembert, mozzarella; four ounces of cottage, farmer, pot, ricotta

Fats and oils: butter, margarine, oils, shortening, and real mayonnaise in reasonable amounts, to taste (*not* a pound of butter or whole jar of mayonnaise)

Condiments: any amount of salt, pepper, onion, and garlic salt or powder; any dry, granulated spice that does not contain sugar; horseradish, vinegar, powdered or Chinese mustard; up to one tablespoon of regular mustard and Worcestershire sauce

Flavorings: as much vanilla, rum, coconut, and other extracts (available in gourmet shops if not in regular supermarkets) as you like

Heavy cream: six teaspoons

Lemon or lime juice: the juice of one

No No! Foods

1. Bread, flour-containing products, fruits or juices, honey or any sugar-containing products,

vegetables (except for salad ingredients listed)

2. Milk, skimmed milk, yogurt, soup, or dairy substitutes (heavy cream is O.K.)

3. Diet products: candy, milkshakes, fruit, bread, etc.

4. Tomato products, such as catsup or sweet pickles (as in relish)

5. Cough drops, lozenges, or sweetened liquid medications

6. Food that contains fillers or added ingredients in the sugar or starch family; each food must be one hundred percent pure

7. Oysters, clams, mussels, pickled fish such as herring or salmon

8. Liver, sweetbreads, salami, sausage, meatballs, meat loaf, or other meat with filler or stuffing or sauce

All fruit is *out* on the low-carbohydrate diet, and that means cooked fruit, fruit juices, and "diet" canned fruit, too. As Dr. Atkins remarks, "I see pretty girls—a little too plump, but pretty—taking their lunch to the park. And what do they have? Three pieces of fruit. There is a false assumption that fruit has no calories . . . or very few. It not only has calories, but it's also loaded with carbohydrates. The only thing that has more sugar is cake or ice cream loaded with refined sugar!"

"Read the labels on all packaged diet foods," Dr. Atkins warns. " 'Diet' ice cream, ice milk, and cottage cheese actually contain *more* carbohydrates than the nondiet versions. If you see sorbitol or corn-syrup solids on a diet-food label, you're getting an overload of carbohydrates. Diet salad dressings usually contain sugar or corn syrup and most diet sodas, of course, now contain *some* sugar—the amount is listed on the labels.

"Skimmed milk is misleading, too. The makers of skimmed milk are not lying when they say a certain percentage of milk fat has been removed; but, in place of the fat are corn-syrup solids. You're better off drinking coffee with heavy cream."

Here's how to live (and feel) *well* on this diet:

1. Eat whenever you're hungry. Eat as much as you need to stop hunger pangs. After two days you

shouldn't *have* hunger pangs.

2. No meal is mandatory. If you're not hungry, don't eat.

3. One ounce of alcoholic beverage is allowed throughout the diet (Dr. Atkins suggests you save it for Saturday night). Remember, the diet is for only ten days, and abstinence is worth it.

4. Be gourmet—have cheese for dessert. Or, try Dr. Atkins's Piña Colada Seduction Dessert. (See recipe below.)

5. Salt your food generously, because a rapid weight loss *can* cause salt depletion and weakness.

6. You may want to take a laxative because of the abrupt diet change. Be sure to read the labels and choose one *without* sugar.

Dr. Atkins says: "See a doctor before you start on any diet plan and ask him to give you a glucose tolerance test. Since carbohydrates have a direct impact on blood sugar (glucose), the limitation of carbohydrates can well affect physical fatigue as well as emotional responses," says the doctor. "I believe that half the people who go to their doctors and complain of being run down actually are suffering from a low-blood-sugar disorder.

"So many girls bolt down a chocolate bar for quick energy, but when a chocolate bar instantly charges you up from droopiness to high energy there is undoubtedly a metabolic imbalance. Tiredness should be in direct proportion to exertion; the body has its own mechanism for keeping energy constant. The glucose tolerance test is not complicated, but it stretches over five or six hours so that the blood can be tested at intervals to see if there are rapid changes in blood sugar. That's why most doctors don't want to bother, so *you* be sophisticated enough to *insist* on it."

Dr. Atkins's Piña Colada Seduction Dessert
(serves two)

"Lovemaking," says Dr. Atkins, "is the best dessert of all. This recipe is for 'afters'—after dinner, after the movies, after listening to music, after the lovemaking!"

4 oz. fresh ricotta cheese
Ice cubes

Flavor extracts: pineapple, rum, coconut, banana (optional)

Liquid Sucaryl with cyclamates (from drugstore; ordinary Sucaryl produces a slightly bitter taste)

Knox's unflavored gelatin (optional)

1. Crush enough ice cubes to equal the density of the cheese.

2. Combine crushed ice with cheese.

3. Add the pineapple, rum, vanilla, and banana flavorings and liquid Sucaryl to taste.

4. For a more solid, pudding form, add some unflavored Knox's gelatin.

5. Pour into iced glasses and spoon drink.

VOGUE SUPER DIET. This was also developed by Dr. Robert Atkins (who worked out the Cosmo Diet above). You're scheduled to be able to lose ten pounds in sixteen days.

Days 1–4. You can eat any quantity (the less, the better) of the following, *and nothing else:*

Meat: any kind but those mixed with other ingredients (sausage, meatballs, frankfurters, cold cuts)

Fish: any kind but oysters, clams, mussels, and pickled fish

Eggs and Fowl: any kind

Salads: 2 small green salads ($\frac{1}{2}$ cup) per day. Use oil and vinegar dressing, with spices and herbs, or grated cheese. Permissible salad ingredients include olives, celery, chicory, Chinese cabbage, cucumber, endive, escarole, leeks, lettuce, onion, pickles, pimento, peppers, radishes, scallions, and watercress.

Cheese: 4 oz. of any hard, aged cheese (such as cheddar, Swiss); no soft cheese or spread

Liquid: water, club soda, bouillon, diet soda, coffee (maximum 4 cups a day), tea, decaffeinated coffee

Butter: any butter, margarine, oil, shortening, or mayonnaise (small portions)

Condiments: salt, pepper, mustard, horseradish, vinegar, vanilla (and all extracts), artificial sweeteners, sugarless spices

Desserts: dietetic gelatin

Days 5–8. You may eat all of the above, plus:

4-oz. vegetable serving (anything you can think of except peas, potatoes, beans, corn, carrots)

1 scoop cottage cheese

1 ounce heavy cream

Days 9–12. All of the above, plus:

oysters, clams, mussels

wine in cooking, or 1 glass dry table wine with dinner, or 1 small portion of fruit a day ($\frac{1}{4}$ cantaloupe, $\frac{1}{2}$ apple, $\frac{1}{2}$ grapefruit)

unlimited cottage cheese

Days 13–16. All of the above, plus:

1 fruit, or 6 oz. tomato juice

1 wine, or 2 oz. vodka, gin, or whiskey

sour cream in recipes

No-No's

beans, bread, candy, catsup, cereal, chewing gum, corn, crackers, ice cream, macaroni, milk, potatoes, rice, spaghetti, sugar

DIET - CUM - GROUP - THERAPY PROGRAMS (WEIGHT WATCHERS, ET AL.) Extremely popular, these long-range diet regimens seem to be the cleverest and most effective that exist. They play on the same basic psychology as once-a-week visits to your family doctor—reinforcement, sympathy, friendly scolding—but hold deeper value because you're dealing with your peers, other Fat Souls, all in the same foodaholic boat. At the group sessions everybody weighs in, you confess your self-delusions and cheating ("I ate a cherry strudel last Tuesday"), talk about discouragements. You learn to laugh at yourself, to get rid of the isolation and shame that most plumpies feel about our cravings. What you receive is encouragement, not nagging. Failures don't exist—only "errors in judgment." Celebration plays a big part in this method; every banished pound is given a rousing send-off. Often members call each other at home for help through moments of impulse when the pecan pie must be devoured. Since everyone's on exactly the same diet, the group becomes a learning trip as well—an exchange of diet hints, recipes, mutual experiences. ("I thought I was the only one in the world who could consume an entire devil's-food cake at one sitting.") For most groups, you must be at least ten pounds overweight to join. More about Weight Watchers in Chapter 11.

SAMPLE CALORIE-COUNTING DIET. Try it for a week. (It's a 1,000-calorie-a-day diet, which means you'll probably lose about two pounds weekly, the most you can expect from a reasonable, long-term diet plan.) If you make substitutes, you *must* first consult your calorie chart: Two ounces of shrimp *do not* have the same calorie count as two of lamb. Incidentally, all references to coffee assume you're drinking it black or with artificial sweetener only— *no* cream or milk.

First Day

Breakfast
   ½ grapefruit
   1 boiled egg
   1 slice rye toast
   ½ cup skim milk
   coffee or tea

Lunch
   ½ cup tomato juice
   American cheese sandwich (2 slices cheese, 2 slices white toast, mustard, and lettuce)
   1 peach
   ¼ cup skim milk
   coffee or tea

Dinner
   1 cup bouillon
   2 oz. broiled halibut or other fish
   ½ cup spaghetti with tomato sauce
   ½ cup cooked carrots
   celery sticks
   1 plum
   ¼ cup skim milk
   coffee or tea

Bedtime Nibble
   1 cup skim milk
   3 soda crackers

Second Day

Breakfast
   ½ cup apple juice
   ½ cup cooked wheat cereal
   ½ cup skim milk

1 scrambled egg
coffee or tea

Lunch

2 oz. tuna fish with 1 teaspoon mayonnaise
$\frac{1}{2}$ cup tossed salad with tomato and lemon
1 small roll
2 unsweetened peach halves
$\frac{1}{4}$ cup skim milk
coffee or tea

Dinner

2 oz. roast lamb
$\frac{1}{2}$ cup green peas
1 small baked potato
1 tablespoon butter
cold asparagus on lettuce with lemon
$\frac{1}{2}$ cup unsweetened fruit cocktail
$\frac{1}{4}$ cup skim milk
coffee or tea

Bedtime Nibble

1 cup skim milk
2 plain graham crackers

Why not try—with the help of your trusty calorie counter—to construct the next four diet days yourself? You see basically how it's done: a very substantial breakfast, many small portions of a great variety of dishes, an emphasis on vegetables. If you work in an office, lunches will probably be most problematic. Arrange them so you can bring everything from home, or plan items available at your local coffee shop or delicatessen. If you're really industrious and honest, with a wizard head for arithmetic, make substitutions: Perhaps you'd rather skip the bread at lunch, have an equivalent extra of cottage cheese. O.K.—but no cribbing.

WORKING GIRL'S HAMBURGER DIET (Lose Ten Pounds in Two Weeks.) It *is* true that some diets are easier to follow than others. Diets are difficult when they are too expensive (filet mignon all the way), too bothersome (prepare a third of a cup celery tops, one-and-a-half-inch lengths of asparagus, and a piece of beef measuring 3 inches by $2\frac{1}{4}$ inches by 1 inch), too inflexible (you must have A for breakfast, B for lunch, C for dinner), or because they leave you starved (six prunes three times a day), or most of all in your case, they are simply too difficult to follow if you are a working girl who has lunch in coffee shops or luncheonettes and has neither the time nor the inclination to spend the whole day preparing dinner.

This diet eliminates all those obstacles, which means you'll have no excuse for quitting once you've begun. The breakfasts are easy to prepare, the lunches readily available, the dinners simple but delicious. It also allows for dinner dates—four during the two-week dieting period—based on menus at typical restaurants (like French, Italian, Chinese) to which you might go.

Instead of chaining yourself to an inflexible program, you can mix and match basic breakfasts, lunches, and dinners to suit yourself in any situation, almost as you would combine separates in your wardrobe. Plan each day's meals with an eye toward variety in tastes and textures—and please be sure to allow yourself only one breakfast, one lunch, and one dinner a day—girl scout's honor.

Though this diet is more flexible than most, it does mean exactly what it says. *You may eat anything on it, but you may not eat anything not included here.* For example, although it says that you may have a pear, a peach, half a grapefruit, or half a cantaloupe, it does not say anything about an apple or a banana, which means you may not have either. A lamb chop is not a pork chop, steak is not pot roast, New England clam chowder is not an acceptable substitute for Manhattan clam chowder.

Do not skip meals. If you do, you will become so hungry you will stuff yourself silly at the next meal and nothing will be gained—or in this case, lost.

We counted calories, so you needn't worry. By selecting the meals as described, you will have about 1,000 calories a day. The diet is high in protein with a moderate amount of fat, but as few carbohydrates as seem practical.

If you follow this diet faithfully, if you are at least ten pounds overweight, and if your body does not retain fluid at an abnormal rate, you will lose the promised ten pounds in the allotted time. Do be sure to check in with your doctor before starting this (or any other) diet to be sure it is safe for your particular physical condition. Do not start to weigh yourself until you have dieted for three days, then do so undressed, first thing in the norming. Don't be discouraged if you slip back a pound or two now and then, or if you don't lose weight for a day or two.

You must not break the continuity of the diet with weekend splurges. Its success is based on fourteen consecutive days and *if you go astray for even one day, you have to start all over.*

Daily Program. Mix and match meals to your heart's desire, except for days when you will have dinner out. In those cases, confine your selection to the menus listed under Dining Out.

Each day select: one breakfast, one lunch, and one dinner from the menus below. *Plus:* Have either eight ounces of tomato juice, or half a grapefruit, or half a cantaloupe—with any one meal or once daily as a between-meal pickup. You may also have eight ounces of skim milk, buttermilk, or yogurt—with any one meal, or once between meals, or before bed.

Include one egg in one of the meals you select. Also be sure to include four to six ounces of calf's liver at least once each week.

You may also add these optional aids to your daily food intake—if you feel you *have* to, but not if you don't:

Diet crackers. Metrecal wafers or any similar cellulose cracker that provides bulk. Take one between meals if you're hungry, before a meal to avoid overeating, or before bed. Carry a couple wrapped in foil in your purse. These crackers should be taken with one of the beverages listed below.

Diet drinks. As much as you want of low-calorie sodas and cola drinks, beef and chicken broth made from dehydrated cubes or powder, clam juice and water. Have all you want, all day long. Ditto coffee and tea without cream or sugar. Use artificial sweeteners if you want them.

Diet fruits. A fresh peach or pear, or three fresh apricots, or eight fresh strawberries without cream or sugar, or an additional half a grapefruit or half a cantaloupe can be added to the basic fruit requirement for the day.

Diet vegetables. Raw carrots (never cooked), celery, cucumber, tomatoes, and lettuce are O.K. for nibbling. Radishes and olives are not.

Diet Breakfasts. No fruit is included in any of these breakfasts. If you feel that breakfast is incomplete without fruit or juice, add half a grapefruit, half a cantaloupe, or four to eight ounces of tomato juice to any of the menus below. If you prefer, skip the fruit for breakfast and add it as an appetizer or a dessert for lunch or dinner, or as a between-meal pickup. Although melba toast and RyKrisp wafers are indicated as substitutes for bacon in these breakfasts, the bacon is a much better idea if you will go to the very slight bother that cooking bacon requires. The protein and fat keep your stomach busy much longer than the toast will, and therefore ward off hunger. Above all, do not skip breakfast entirely. Even a small amount of protein in the morning can prevent almost insatiable midafternoon hunger pangs.

ONE
1 egg, any style, or $\frac{1}{2}$ cup cottage cheese

1 slice crisp bacon, or 1 slice melba toast or RyKrisp

Coffee or tea

TWO
$\frac{1}{4}$ pound lean beef hamburger

Coffee or tea

THREE
2 slices crisp bacon

1 Melozot or Metrecal wafer

Coffee or tea

FOUR
Weekend Brunch (for a day when you will have only one other meal)

Hamburger on horseback ($\frac{1}{4}$ pound lean beef hamburger topped with poached or fried egg and capers)

$1\frac{1}{2}$ slices buttered toast

Coffee or tea

FIVE
Breakfast-in-a-Glass. We devised this diet breakfast for girls who are too busy to cook first thing in the morning, or who just can't stand the idea of

doing so. It's as quick and easy to drink as it is to prepare, high in food value and low in calories.

Combine 8 ounces skim milk, 1 raw egg yolk (no white, please), $\frac{1}{4}$ teaspoon vanilla extract, and, if you like, a few drops artificial sweetener. Mix until frothy in a blender or cocktail shaker. Pour into a chilled glass and dust with nutmeg. To vary the flavor, omit vanilla and substitute almond extract, a little strong black coffee, or an ounce or two of sherry. (Skip the sherry if it leaves you too light-headed to function.) You may also have coffee or tea.

Seven Workday Lunches. Any girl who works for a living will find the menus below easy to follow. They are geared to the standard fare you'll find in most coffee shops and luncheonettes. They're all easy on your caloric and monetary budgets and can be ordered at a counter or table without making you conspicuous or creating an uproar with the waitress. No one will guess you are dieting unless you say so. If you are asked to a special luncheon—a business date or an office celebration—simply switch lunch and dinner menus for that day. Although there are only seven menus here, considering the variety of egg preparations you may order and the choice of three salads permitted in Lunch Three, you have more than enough selections to see you through the ten working days you will live through on this diet.

ONE

$\frac{1}{4}$ pound lean beef hamburger, no roll or bread

1 tomato, with or without lettuce, French dressing (optional)

Coffee or tea

TWO

2 eggs, any style, including Western, ham, cheese or vegetable omelets

2 slices bacon, unless you have had them for breakfast, but not with the omelets above

Coffee or tea

THREE

Shrimp, chicken, or crabmeat salad (1 cup), with mayonnaise

1 tomato with lettuce (If it seems more interesting you can have this as a stuffed tomato surprise.)

Coffee or tea

FOUR

1 cup cottage cheese

Fresh strawberries (about 8), no cream or sugar, or ½ cantaloupe

Coffee or tea

FIVE

Sandwich lunch

Bacon, lettuce, and tomato on toast, no mayonnaise or butter

Coffee or tea

SIX

Quick shopping-day lunch

1 bowl of Manhattan clam chowder or vegetable soup

1 diet cracker

SEVEN

2 frankfurters, no roll or bread

Sauerkraut (optional)

Coffee or tea

With a little practice you should be able to hold the frankfurter with its roll but eat only the meat. That way you do not have to ask for a fork and plate or create a general to-do. If possible, try to find a place that serves all-beef frankfurters, as they are least fattening. The frankfurters should be the thin type, three to four inches in length.

Ten Diet Dinners. (Prepare these yourself from standard recipes in any good cookbook:)

ONE

Cup of clam broth with lemon

1 herb-broiled breast of chicken

Grilled tomato (1) with Parmesan cheese

Green salad, oil and vinegar dressing

Coffee or tea

TWO

1 large veal scallopini sautéed in butter, served with lemon and capers

String-bean salad, dill dressing (1 cup)

Sautéed mushrooms and onions (½ to ¾ cup)

Coffee or tea

THREE

Cup of chicken or beef consommé with minced parsley

2 grilled trout with cucumbers

Asparagus with lemon butter (8 to 10)
Coffee or tea

FOUR

Cup of hot tomato-clam broth

1 cold boiled lobster ($\frac{3}{4}$ pound) or shrimp salad (8 to 10 shrimp) with mayonnaise

Mixed vegetables vinaigrette on lettuce leaves

2 slices melba toast or 2 rye wafers

Coffee or tea

FIVE

Broiled grapefruit half with sherry

Minute steak (6 ounces)

Watercress

Tomato, cucumber, and green pepper salad with oregano, oil, and lemon dressing

Coffee or tea

SIX

Sautéed calf liver (1 slice) with 1 slice crisp bacon

Chopped spinach with butter and nutmeg (1 cup)

Raw carrots and celery sticks

Coffee or tea

SEVEN

2 broiled lamb chops, well trimmed of fat

Zucchini cooked with tomatoes (1 cup)

Broiled mushroom caps (3 large)

Coffee or tea

EIGHT

Broiled fillet of sole (1 large) or 8 broiled large shrimps

Hot or cold broccoli with oil-and-lemon dressing (1 cup)

$\frac{1}{2}$ cup cooked rice

Coffee or tea

NINE

Company dinner

Cup of chicken consommé with egg drops

Roast chicken stuffed with parsley and tarragon (2 slices of white meat for you)

Raw-spinach salad with red onion rings, French dressing

Rice pilaf ($\frac{1}{2}$ cup cooked for you)

Strawberries in white wine (no sugar on yours)
Coffee or tea

TEN

No-cook dinner

2 or 3 slices cold roast beef (Buy about $\frac{1}{4}$ pound at the delicatessen.)

6 artichoke hearts vinaigrette (from a jar) tossed with a cut-up tomato

Fruit (as allowed)

Coffee or tea

Dining Out. Dinner in some wonderful restaurant usually offers more temptation than the average dieter can resist. Of course, you could always order broiled or chopped steak, chicken, or fillet of sole, but who wants to? For one thing, you might as well hold up a flashing neon sign that says, "I'M DIETING!"; for another, you'll wind up feeling frustrated and cheated. It *is* perfectly possible to dine out *deliciously* and still stay within the confines of your fourteen-day program. We have planned diet dinners based on standard menus you'll find in French, Italian, German, Chinese, Middle Eastern, seafood, and steak restaurants. Four such dinners are a maximum for the two-week period, however, and since these meals will inevitably have more calories than dinners you prepare at home, we have compensated in the lunches you may have on those days.

In most cases, you may have an appetizer as well as an entrée. Desserts are completely taboo unless you have not had your daily fruit allowance, in which case you may order it now. Remember that the only fruits permissible are half a grapefruit, half a cantaloupe, eight strawberries without cream or sugar, a fresh pear or peach, or three fresh apricots.

Limit yourself to two drinks and then only if you *must* have them. Two glasses of dry red or white wine, or two whiskeys (any kind) with soda or water, or one before-dinner whiskey and one glass of wine with your food is all you may have. After-dinner brandies and liqueurs, mixed drinks, and aperitif wines such as sherry, Madeira, and vermouth are out for the duration of the diet.

On the days you plan to have dinner out, choose breakfasts and lunches from the following list, adding your fruit allowance as described where-ever you like:

Breakfast. Choose from Breakfasts one, three, or four.

Lunch. If you have Breakfast one or three: a quarter-pound lean hamburger, no roll or bread; one sliced tomato, with or without lettuce, no dressing; coffee or tea. If you have Breakfast four: two eggs, any style, or a cup of cottage cheese, or a hard-boiled egg and half a cup cottage cheese; a sliced tomato, with or without lettuce, no dressing; coffee or tea

French Dinner
Appetizers (optional)
Artichoke vinaigrette
Mussels rémoulade (6)
Escargots (6)
Celery rémoulade
Entrées
Coq au vin
Veal or chicken marengo
Paupiette de veau
Calves' brains au beurre noir
Filet of sole, sauté meunière
Bouillabaisse
Grilled entrecôte
Escargots (12)
Roast lamb (gigot) without traditional beans
Beef bourguignon (if you skip an appetizer)
Salad or Vegetables (optional)
Green leafy vegetable without sauce, or mixed green salad with vinaigrette dressing
No dessert
French or American coffee
Pitfalls to Avoid: Onion soup with its bread-and-cheese topping; bread, especially for the sauces and escargot butter; the wonderful duck prepara-tions; the crisp pommes frites; all desserts

Italian Dinner
Appetizers (optional)
Roast peppers and anchovies
Artichoke (if it is not stuffed with bread or bread crumbs)

Baked clams casino (6)
Broiled shrimp, scampi style (3 or 4)
Entrées
Veal paillard
Veal rollatini
Veal and peppers
Chicken cacciatora
Calf liver Veneziana
Beef braciole (if you skip an appetizer)
Steak alla pizzaiola (if you skip an appetizer)
Broiled shrimp, scampi style (8–10)
Clams or mussels marinara
Zuppa de pesce (a mixed fish soup similar to bouillabaisse)
Salad or Vegetables (optional)
Sautéed or steamed spinach, broccoli, zucchini, or green salad, string-bean salad, or tomatoes with basil
No dessert
Espresso or American coffee
Pitfalls to Avoid: All of the luscious soups, pastas, and risottos; bread, especially for the sauces; fried meats and vegetables that are breaded; desserts

German Dinner (One drink is the limit here.)
Appetizers (optional)
Herring salad
Head cheese (Sulze)
Ochsenmaul salad or any meat salad
Entrées
Naturschnitzel (an unbreaded version of the veal Wiener schnitzel)
Chicken in the pot (if you do not eat noodles or dumplings)
Boiled beef (if you skip an appetizer)
Blue-cooked trout
Tartar steak
Roast veal (wiener rostbraten)
Deutsch beefsteak (chopped steak)
Königsberger klops with sauerkraut (a sort of meatball dumpling)
Salad or Vegetables (optional)
Sauerkraut, red cabbage, pickled beets, cucumbers in vinegar, green pepper salad
No dessert

Coffee

Pitfalls to Avoid: All of the great soups; the whole array of dumplings, noodles, potato pancakes, and puddings; bread; wursts; lentil and bean dishes; fried meats that are breaded; the sensational cakes and pastries; beer

Chinese Dinner (One drink is the limit here.)
Appetizers
None
Entrées
Egg foo yong (meat and vegetable omelet)
Moo goo gai pan (sliced chicken with green vegetable)
Pepper steak (beef and green peppers)
Lung hai gai kew (lobster and chicken with vegetables)
Any chow mein (if you can eat between the noodles)
Shrimp with lobster sauce (if you can bear it without rice)
Lobster cantonese (again, riceless)
No dessert
Tea

Pitfalls to Avoid: All soups (thickened with cornstarch); appetizers such as spareribs, egg roll, breaded fried shrimp; wontons, noodles, and rice; canned and preserved fruits

Middle Eastern Dinner
Appetizers (optional)
Artichoke heart (1 large, 2 small)
Eggplant and tomato salad
Stuffed mussels (3)
Stuffed grape leaves (2)
Entrées
Shish kebab
Roast chicken
Moussaka (eggplant baked with ground lamb)
Any lamb and vegetable stew
Vegetables (optional)
Sautéed or stewed green vegetable or eggplant
No dessert
American coffee

Pitfalls to Avoid: Rich soups; rice or cracked

wheat pilafs; lentil and bean dishes; the wonderful Arabic flat bread; the luscious flaky pastries; sugared Turkish coffee

Seafood Dinner
Appetizers (optional)
Clams or oysters on the half-shell (6)
Shrimp cocktail (6)
Cup of clam broth
Entrées
Any broiled or steamed fish or shellfish (except mackerel, bluefish, swordfish, salmon, shad, whitefish, or butterfish)
Salad (optional)
Mixed green salad, oil-and-vinegar dressing
No dessert
Coffee or tea
Pitfalls to Avoid: Thick, creamy chowders; crackers, biscuits and bread; French-fried potatoes; breaded fried fish; au gratin dishes; desserts

Steakhouse Dinner
Although this might seem to be one of the best choices for a dieter, it is not if you order a tremendous steak. A one-pound steak has more calories than you're supposed to have in a day, hence the following alternates:
Appetizers (optional)
Shrimp, clam, or oyster cocktail (6)
Entrées
Broiled half-chicken
2 thin, lean slices of roast beef
Calf liver
Chopped steak
Minute or sliced steak
Two lamb chops
Salad or Vegetables
Steamed, green leafy vegetable; broiled mushrooms; sliced tomatoes; green salad, oil-and-vinegar dressing
No dessert
Coffee
Pitfalls to Avoid: Huge steaks; French-fried onion rings; potatoes; bread; rich salad dressings; desserts; beer

THE BRITISH LOSE-A-STONE-A-WEEK DIET.

There comes a time in every girl's life when she would cheerfully swap her country's atomic secrets (were they in her keeping) for a foolproof method of taking off fifteen pounds in one week. A yo-yo-dieter friend of mine used to have many such moments— the most memorable at 7:30 P.M. on the eve of a Sudden Important Date, when she discovered to her horror that half the clothes in her wardrobe were too tight and the rest were—aaagh!—size fourteen.

She decided something had to be done, and fast. She *could* have gone on one of the diets that were pasted carefully into her recipe scrapbook: sweet-and-sour salad; eggs and grapefruit; cottage cheese—all of which worked beautifully for her until about Day Three, when she went berserk, ate everything in sight, and gained back all she'd lost and a few pounds as well. But she happened to be in England then, so instead, she went to a health farm.

The nearest American equivalent to an English health farm would probably be Elizabeth Arden's Maine Chance, or the Golden Door in California, which are designed to change wealthy, flabby women to lovely young sylphs—at seven-hundred fifty dollars or more a week. But British health farms are designed for everybody—rich and not so rich, old and young, male and female, fat and thin. Rather than try to make you glamorous, they try to make you healthy; but if you want to lose weight quickly, you can whip off a stone (fourteen pounds) or more in one week.

It was at a health farm that James Bond nearly met death on a vibrating machine in *Thunderball;* it was at a health farm that Vidal Sassoon proposed (over a lemon juice for two) to the girl he married, and it was at a health farm that Lynn Redgrave shed all those extra pounds she had put on for the movie *Georgy Girl.*

Thousands of Londoners (models, secretaries, executives, actresses, nurses, teachers, accountants, and tycoons) make a regular practice of spending a week at a health farm every few months—at prices ranging from thirty-five pounds (eighty-seven dollars) to ninety pounds (two hundred and twenty-four dollars) a week.

My friend chose Grayshott Hall, England's newest and most luxurious spa. She went there mainly because Grayshott offers an Executive Weekend Special—you arrive Wednesday at twelve noon, fat, and leave Sunday noon, seven pounds lighter. (She thought that with a seven-pound start, she'd have the incentive to lose the rest herself.)

For those who are wondering if the British health-farm methods can be duplicated by an American girl at home, here's the diary she kept during her stay:

Wednesday, Day #1. This place is incredible! Grayshott Hall was formerly the baronial home of Lord Tennyson, to which has been added a lavish new fifty-room wing and a heated indoor pool. There are also a nine-hole golf course, man-made lake, tennis courts, and seven hundred acres of the only wilderness I have seen in England.

Arrived today at noon by train to the nearest village. I had bravely eaten a grapefruit half for breakfast, and figured I wouldn't get anything else for four days. Unfortunately, I somehow managed to miss my train stop and got lost in the middle of Surrey. In the ensuing complications, I had a trauma and, what was worse, that favorite British snack, a Cadbury's Fruit and Nut Bar.

And so my taxi pulled into the great circular driveway of scenic Grayshott Hall. Rolls-Royces and Bentleys in profusion. I was staggered by the reception room: all marble, crystal chandeliers, red carpet, and Regency furnishings. They told me that my "consultation" wouldn't be until 3 P.M., and to have lunch in the dining room.

The dining room is more red plush, sunshine, and crystal. Lunch—or, rather, dinner—is about twenty-two huge wooden bowls filled with different kinds of salad, set out in a lavish smorgasbord. Weird combinations such as cauliflower and pineapple, grated carrot and coconut, melon and green pepper—all gorgeous. For dessert: an enormous dish of Grayshott's homemade yogurt topped with honey and wheat germ. The Fruit and Nut Bar weighed heavily on my conscience, not to mention my digestion.

There is a boutique here selling fashions by some of London's top houses—Hardy Amies, John Cavanagh, and Clive. All size eight!

Oh, yes, the rest of the inmates (patients? clients? customers?): a lot of very wealthy people including a few supersleek women who are much older than they look, one girl about my age, some pudgy young men, and four doctors.

I went to my room for a nap. There was a knock at the door, and a little silver pitcher arrived with a note attached: PLEASE LEAVE URINE SPECIMEN ON FIRST MORNING ONLY BY 7:30 A.M., PLEASE. Who are they trying to kid? I have never been able to get up at 7:30 in my *life*.

At 3 P.M., I went down to see Mr. Burt, who is my osteopathic nature-cure specialist. As instructed, I was wearing my bra, pants, and dressing gown. I had been wearing my new turquoise jungle-flowered bikini outfit, but thought I had better switch to something discreet and beige for the good Mr. Burt.

Thank goodness. Mr. Burt turned out to be thirty, and a bachelor. We had a lengthy chat, during which he told me all about Bernarr McFadden, who started this whole cult. "It's his one-hundred-and-tenth birthday this month," he told me. "Wow," I said. "I'm converted."

"Unfortunately," Mr. Burt said, with a melancholy look, "he won't be around to celebrate it. He died at eighty-six."

I was murmuring my condolences while Mr. Burt explained that McFadden should have lived to 120: "It was all his wife's fault; he married her at eighty and she was a bad influence. He went on the rails and started *eating*."

Oh, horrors, I gasped.

Mr. Burt asked me a number of questions. Like, what do I have for breakfast? (Just a little fruit, and sometimes an egg and a piece of toast.) Lunch? (A salad with very little dressing.) Dinner? (Meat, a salad, and one vegetable. No potatoes.)

It wasn't until afterward that I realized that the past Sunday dinner consisted of a bottle of wine, two sandwiches, chocolate-chip cookies, a chocolate cupcake, and another Fruit and Nut Bar. Monday dinner was two gin Collinses, a Playboy Club steak (midget and very well tanned), French fries, a dill pickle, and garlic bread.

"Do you drink?" Burt asked. "Only occasionally," I told him virtuously.

And how about white sugar? "Good grief, no!" I exclaimed. Truthfully. (What kind of sugar do you suppose they put in chocolate-chip cookies and Fruit and Nut Bars?)

So, he examined me, told me I am perfectly healthy except that I have lousy posture and am a few pounds overweight—all of which I knew already. Then, he told me that I have yellow cholesterol deposits in my eyes. Help! So, no more cholesterol foods for a while.

By this time, I don't want anything to eat. Ever again. I want to be *pure*. Supper tonight consisted of a hunk of melon and a pear.

Thursday, Day #2. Breakfast of hot "lemon water" and half a grapefruit arrived at 7:30, along with all the morning papers. And, surprise, I had been up and ready, stomach growling, for about a half-hour.

The grapefruit was followed by a visit from Mr. Moule, the osteopath (known as a chiropractor in the U.S.A.) who runs Grayshott Hall. Mr. Moule, thin, distinguished, and gray-haired, also edits a British health magazine, *Here's Health.*

Mr. Moule made it clear to me that Grayshott Hall is a *health center*, not a reducing center. The "nature-cure" method by fasting, which he advocates, is for everybody, not merely the fatties. When a person stops eating temporarily, he told me, all the energy normally used in digestion is used to eliminate all the toxic elements stored up over many years. This fasting often has such side effects as dizziness, fainting, and nausea. Nothing to *worry* about, he said; it simply means that all the "toxins" are being eliminated.

He is such a nice, sincere man that he nearly convinced me—until I picked up a copy of his magazine, *Here's Health*, and read one of his articles, "The Facts About Fasting." (Quote: "It is significant that surviving victims of Nazi concentration camps were found to be free from any of their former organic diseases.'')

Most people who come here spend three days fasting on lemon juice, eliminating old toxic remnants of hamburgers, martinis, pancakes and maple syrup, pizza, lox and cream cheese on bagels. Then they graduate to grapefruit, yogurt, and other delicacies. Everyone gets a different diet, depending on the ailment. In addition, they are given sauna baths, massages, chiropractic treatment, and such funny things as colonic irrigation, which is sort of a high-powered enema, and sitz baths in which you sit in hot water with your feet in cold water and vice versa.

Fortunately, I only want to lose a few pounds and am writing an article besides, which means my menu is: Breakfast: Half grapefruit and lemon water. Lunch: All the salad I can eat. Dinner: Small piece of fruit.

We're segregated according to our diets. People in the dining room get to *eat;* those of us in the "Light Diet Room" snarl at each other over our grapefruits or Biobalm (slippery-elm-bark powder mixed with milk, and then heated).

There are two treatment rooms; the one with the pink door is for girls. I had my first session today: an Oriental massage by a Japanese angel with two dozen fingers; then a salt shower, sauna, and nap.

Tonight at supper, I met Linda. She is Michael Caine's agent, a girl of about twenty-three with a beautiful face, fifty pounds of surcharge, and such a captivating personality that you just don't notice. With her great floppy fake eyelashes and Twiggy makeup, she keeps the Light Diet Room laughing, while managing to exist on three half-grapefruits a day.

There are many people here who *could* be interesting. But unfortunately conversation is confined to who's eating what, how many minutes everybody is getting in the sauna, and how so-and-so lost three stone on hot water alone last year at Enton Hall—which is a place similar to Grayshott, only *more* Spartan.

Friday, Day #3. This evening, as Linda and I were walking to the village, one of the inmates—

82

the one whom we have christened Aging Playboy —came by in his Bentley and said why didn't we go to this lovely inn he knew of for tomato juice? Why not? So we sat in the back of the Bentley, pushing buttons to make the windows go up and down, rather like underprivileged children, and finally arrived at an old English hostel called Frensham Pond Inn. To our dismay, Aging Playboy sat there and drank a full bottle of champagne (Veuve Clicquot, 1955) while we sipped our V-8. Then, he ordered a *dressed crab* to be served in the dining room, and asked if we wanted to watch him eat it. Or would we care to join him in a small, er, nibble?

I finally weakened and had a steak. Medium rare. It was magnificent.

Saturday, Day #4. Miracle of miracles. Have lost five pounds, steak and all. ("It speeded up your metabolism," Linda keeps insisting to me.)

The whole nature-cure ritual has evolved into a religion here. Mr. Moule is God and has laid down these commandments: Thou shalt not have too much protein, or use salt, drink alcohol, plain water, coffee, or milk, use white sugar, white flour, or eat more than four eggs a week. If you do any of these things, you die a slow death by poisoning.

Mr. Burt has become a kind of sainted martyr. "Do you know," one lady told me, with awe and admiration, "he fasts one day *every week*."

Gossip here is *rife*. Not about anything so trite as sex. Over tea today, Mrs. A told Mrs. B that Mr. C had been spotted coming out of Miss D's room after lights out. Fascinated, Mrs. B leaned forward and asked, "What do you suppose they were *eating*?"

The only moral code is over who is "cheating" and who isn't. Who has a box of chocolates in his room and nibbles them in a secret orgy every night? Who went to Frensham Pond Inn for a cream tea? Who went down to the village and demolished a basket of strawberries, two pears, six plums, and a bunch of grapes?

Then there are the games, like "Who's Cheating the Diet Chart?" After supper (a slice of honeydew melon and a small bunch of grapes) we play "Scavenger Hunt," which means: (1) If there are any old lemon slices from the lemon water lying about, we fight over them; (2) some kinds of melon can be scraped almost to the rind. I almost slashed my wrists tonight when I realized they had taken away my melon rind and I had missed out on a good two tablespoons of scrapings.

"When I Get Out" is when we sit around and talk about all the things we are going to eat when our penance is up. Like gefilte fish, matzo-ball soup, Dover sole in cream sauce, tagliatelle, and Yorkshire pudding with gravy. But when *I* get out, it's going to be prune and grapefruit salad, because I really am *so* good.

Sunday, Discharge Day. After one of Grayshott's opulent salad smorgasbords (including a jacket potato), I checked out—exactly a half-stone (seven pounds) lighter than when I went in. I feel thin, glamorous, confident, energetic. I'm convinced I will have no trouble at all losing the other seven pounds.

P.S. One Week Later. I hate to spoil this lovely success story, but the day I got back, everything went *black.* I dimly remember Mr. Moule's "No's": No grilled-cheese sandwiches, French fries, cookies, scrambled eggs and bacon, tall glasses of milk, ice-cream cones, potato chips, and other shocking things. This morning, I discovered I had gained back every one of those lost Grayshott pounds. Deciding that maybe I had psychiatric problems, I went to my doctor and blurted out the whole story.

He laughed and said I was *not* a mental case. He told me I was probably suffering from low blood sugar and a lack of protein. The health-farm techniques may work for some people, he said, but I am obviously not one of them. "They don't *reeducate* you in eating," he went on, "so you go back home and revert to your former habits—or worse, because your system craves all that food it's been deprived of."

Then he told me what I should have known already: There is no secret, painless way to get thin, either quickly or slowly. Some foods are fattening; we all know what they are. We "slightly overweights" in particular must be constantly vigilant—against fats, sugars, starches, and that great social-business trap of cocktails.

He gave me a diet sheet with a list of "No's" remarkably similar to Mr. Moule's: *absolutely no* butter, margarine, fat or oil, sugar, jam, marmalade, honey, sweets, chocolate, cocoa, desserts,.ice cream, dried or tinned fruits, nuts, bread (except for one slice daily), milk (except for one glass daily), cake, cookies, toast, patent reducing breads, cereals, oatmeal, barley, rice, macaroni, spaghetti, sausages, cheese, cocktail savories, or alcohol of any sort.

Other than that, I can eat everything I like— which really leaves only fruits, vegetables, and as much as I like of that Grayshott taboo: lean meat, eggs, fish, and poultry. Basically, he said, I would have to follow this plan the rest of my life, if I wanted to stay thin.

"It might take *weeks* to lose that weight," he warned, sending me out the door. "But if you persevere, it will work."

P.P.S. It does.

CHAPTER 11: MY OWN FAVORITE TWENTY-POUND-SHEDDING DIET

When I performed the kind of self-analysis I'm asking you to do—to find the perfect diet for *me*—I realized (after trying just about *everything,* mind you) that I had the following basic needs: Heinzlike variety, a *full* feeling after each meal, and big quantities of fruit. In addition, I had some special requirements: At the time I was traveling a great deal for my work, so I needed a diet that could handle plane fare (the edible kind) and room service; also, I love to cook, and wanted meals more challenging than meat shoved under a flame. To boot, I can't add brilliantly, so calorie counting was obviously out.

My choice—and a superb one *for me*—was the Weight Watchers' diet. (Basically the same program is used by all such groups.) I never attended the sessions because of my traveling, but I followed the diet to the crumb. Here it is, in brief. (For all the details, I suggest you buy Jean Nidetch's *Weight Watchers Cookbook;* Hearthside Press, $4.95.)

On this diet, you don't count calories, but instead weigh portions on a small food scale. You must eat three meals a day. You must eat a minimum of five fish dishes a week (six ounces at dinner, four at lunch), four to seven eggs a week, beef a maximum of three times a week, and liver once. Many foods—primarily vegetables—are unlimited; they may be taken at any time in any quantity. Alcohol, fried foods, gravies, cake, butter, are on the long list of for-biddens. Here's a typical day's menu:

Breakfast

1 egg, or 1 oz. hard cheese, or 2 oz. fish, or $\frac{1}{4}$ cup cottage or pot cheese

1 slice enriched bread

Coffee, tea, etc.

Lunch

4 oz. fish (canned or fresh) or beef or poultry, or 6 oz. cottage cheese, or 2 oz. hard cheese, or 2 eggs

1 slice enriched bread

Unlimited vegetables (asparagus, broccoli, cucumber, green pepper, rhubarb, 21 others)

Dinner

6 oz. fish, meat, or poultry

$\frac{1}{2}$ cup limited vegetables (artichokes, tomato, carrots, eggplant, peas, 13 others)

Unlimited vegetables in unlimited quantity

Each day, you must also include three fruits (one must be grapefruit or orange), and two cups skim milk or buttermilk.

Some strange, arbitrary restrictions pepper this diet. (I disregarded them.) For instance, Mrs. Nidetch insists that eggs be eaten only at breakfast or lunch. Why? Same for the limited vegetables, which are for dinner only. Dietetic foods, with the exception of low-calorie sodas, are never permitted—a rule I never followed because of my passion for dietetic strawberry preserves (great mixed with fresh rhubarb or as topping for farmer cheese on toast!)

These rules, apparently, have no dietary or nutritional purpose; they're supposed to discipline the dieter. The diet's psychology is: enough freedom to keep eating joyful, enough rigidity to make lapses difficult. The ban on dietetic foods is due to Mrs. Nidetch's personal distaste for products with chemical additives.

Some people turn off this diet because they hate weighing foods on the little postage scale. I found this rule a painful duty for about one week. By then my eye had adjusted to what six ounces of bluefish looks like, and in restaurants I knew automatically how much fish was resting on my plate.

Alas, nothing in life is flawless, and this diet has other drawbacks, even for me. I *don't* adore fish, and would like to be able to eat more meat, grander portions. I could easily live forever without milk. On the good side, if you're a night snacker like me, you can save all the fruit allotments for after dinner. And you're allowed wide menu variety in restaurants, satisfying nibbles any time of day or night. Most important of all, this diet lets me use my creative cookery to its loftiest peaks, and I don't really feel like a dieter . . . well, not *too* much, anyway.

Face it: No diet will ever pacify all our sweet needs or lust for sheer gluttony. It will never keep us from temptation, and will never be easy. If your idea of the Perfect Diet is one that requires no willpower, discipline, or occasional hunger, you are utterly doomed (just as if you were looking for the Perfect Man, who also doesn't exist).

Now, are you closer to discovering the Perfect Diet for you? Talk with your doctor, chat with friends (not the chronic dieting faddists, but the serious weight losers), experiment. Above all, start *now*.

CHAPTER 12: TO DRINK OR NOT TO DRINK

Probably I should have hired an outside expert to write this chapter because—let me tell you right away—I'm not, in my soul of souls, a drinker. I *like* to drink, mind you; I adore champagne and good red wine and Scotch sours and black Russians, but two are plenty. Drinking, too, does not feed any psychological hungers for me, as it does for people who really drink heavily, or who *need* to drink. If, through some insane political regression, they brought back Prohibition tomorrow, I would shrug my shoulders and think about dinner. Unlike some of my imbibing friends, given the caloric choice between an evening of boozing and eating, need I tell you my preference?

However, I know that many of you feel alcohol is important. Since it is also *fattening*, we must deal with it.

If you can give up all spirits for the duration of your diet (that is, if you can without feeling a gigantic, nervous-making vacuum in your life), do it. A glass of champagne, about the cheapest caloric goody, is still 85 calories (more than an apple), and a Tom Collins is 180. Besides, booze doesn't fill you up like apples, but seems to do just the opposite—turn on the appetite button. Three cocktails before dinner not only provide you with anywhere from 300 to 800 calories, but also can make you want to tear down the walls to get at the nearest foodstuffs. Here's what else is bad:

91

Mixers. Killers. Ginger ale, tonic, eggnog, hot toddy, all those yummies with sugar . . . *killers*.

Drinking companions. Just as drinking goes hand-in-glove with smoking (I'm told that by recently reformed smokers who now suffer most at cocktail parties), alcohol also nuzzles closely with peanuts, pretzels, cheese, and pigs-in-blankets—bad companions *all!*

Forgetfulness. If you get tipsy, you may just forget you're on a diet altogether! We all tend to absentmindedness in that dazed state that follows six bloody Marys, and falling off our lovely little diet may be the least embarrassing tumble to recall the morning after.

Hangovers. In case you haven't noticed, hangovers make you famished for sweets.

But for the same reasons that I wouldn't advise a heavy smoker to give up cigarettes while dieting, I think you probably should continue to drink, somewhat, if you're normally a heavy drinker. Otherwise the tension may turn you to food, which will be even more calamitous. You *can* find the Perfect Diet that includes a drink before lunch and dinner, or some dry wine. Unfortunately, *no* diet will let you imbibe to your heart's content. That's the price.

Very few drinkers/dieters know much about alcoholic calories, I've discovered. Many believe a drink is a drink is a drink. They don't have any notion that a glass of dry wine has 55 fewer calories than the same quantity of sweet wine. Or that two glasses of dry white wine have fewer calories than one gin and tonic.

Here's an interesting tidbit volunteered by one of my saloon-going friends: A teaspoon of brandy in your after-dinner coffee contributes relatively few calories, but satisfies almost the same as if it were pure brandy (at 75 calories for one and a half ounces).

In Chapter 18 we'll get to some hints for handling drinking situations when you've decided to give up alcohol *completely* for the duration of your diet.

THE DRINKING GIRL'S DIET. After polling a cast of thousands, we have found that among the few successful dieters is a small genius group—those who have managed significant weight losses on a drink-and-diet regimen. Depending on whether they dropped five or thirty pounds, they all accomplished such losses within comparatively short times—anywhere from three days to three months. In every case (and here's the *news*) these now-thin wonders watched more what they ate than drank, and usually without that miserly martyred feeling that goes along with most hard-core dieting. In some cases the skinnies departed a bit from our basic drinker's diet, which was compiled from the already-proved success stories of the majority. However, we found the successful dieters to be rather high-living, fun-loving types, the kind of people who would give up pastry, but not parties. In general the results show that dieting-and-drinking has to take into account both calories and carbohydrates, and that by sticking to high-protein foods and low-calorie drinks, almost anyone can duplicate our success stories without drinking iced tea at the cocktail hour.

Drinker's Diet

Two to four highballs or cocktails a day (this includes Scotch, gin, vodka, and wine) and all the water you can drink.

Maximum amounts (if you like) of lean meat, chicken, fish, cottage cheese, and eggs.

Maximum amounts of coffee and tea (with artificial sweeteners).

Some amounts of low-calorie sodas, soups, and tomato juice.

Minimal amounts of orange juice, grapefruit, green salads, and cheese.

Nothing else.

That's simple enough, isn't it? And here is a handful of success stories to convince you that a diet *can* work, even if it is *easy*. Notice that the following are all variations of the basic drinker's diet.

Success Story #217: Duluth Girl Makes It Big by Getting Small. There she was, a comfortable 128 pounds, with the face of an angel, the hips and thighs of a bakery owner's daughter (which she was). Though new to New York, everyone told her she ought to be a model, but only a model agency had told her to drop fifteen pounds—fast. In three weeks she had her first assignment, after living on only chicken breasts but all the while putting away up to four bloody Marys a day.

Success Story #402: Susceptible Buyer Abandons Ups and Downs of Old Crash Program. A conscientious, cuddly type, Cheryl P. always felt there was but one kind of diet—starvation. "When I want to lose weight, I want to lose it fast," she said. Strangely, she could thin down in nothing flat, all the while looking wan and wild-eyed; unhappily she was prone to gain it all back at the first sign of a double malted. Her solution: four helpings of Carnation Slender a day—with two pre-"dinner" martinis. Result: twenty pounds gone in four weeks.

Success Story #633: The Case of the Vanishing Publicist. A small-town girl who quickly developed big-city tastes, May B. blossomed from a size eight to a fourteen in only two short years, thanks to unending business lunches and a penchant for Manhattans. After a disastrous session with a lover—"You disgust me," he said—she left him. "He was tactless," she said. But she did some agonizing reevaluating. By sticking to spritzers (white wine and club soda) and eating fish, chicken, and lean meat, May dwindled back to a size eight in only four months. She isn't going to be seen around much anymore—Ms. B.'s moving to London with her new husband, a diplomat.

Success Story #978: Swan Song. Angela M. is not an ugly duckling, but she was a beautiful goose—she looked rather like one from the rear. This was strange because Angela was *always* on a diet. But what she did was jumble up her diets, and her hard drinks were *always* high-calorie drinks. One day she was on an all-the-ice-cream-you-can-eat regimen, the next time it was another perfectly acceptable diet but a different one. In between she liked to have Manhattans (175 calories) and Brandy Alexanders (225 calories). When she discovered the infinite varieties of pleasures on the Drinking Girl's Diet (and stayed with it), she finally began to lose weight. Angela is looking much less ducklike from the back these days.

Success Story #412: Caviar-Prone Editor

Prefers Russian Drinking to Dressing. One of our favorite types—sensible, sensitive, and sincere—is now wearing new suits (his old ones are too big). His main trick: light breakfasts and lunches, and substituting vodka martinis (up to three), pressed caviar, chopped onions, and RyKrisp for dinner two or three nights a week.

Success Story #804: Boutique Owner Keeps Moving. A chic redhead often described as a "little bit of a thing" used to have little bits of her bulging all over. Her diet: No breakfast—she gets up late; eggs for lunch; and nothing barred for dinner. Then after that she goes dancing, at least five nights a week and pretty energetically. She cools off between sets with two to three Scotches. Never has a hangover—in her head or over her chain belt.

Here's how to tell how many calories are in the cocktails you drink. (Liquors *do vary*.) Look for the proof number on your favorite kind of hard liquor. It's approximately the number of calories it contains per ounce. For instance, one ounce of 80-proof vodka has a little fewer than 80 calories. Some dark rums run higher than 150-proof.

From 70–80 calories per ounce: gin, Scotch, rye, vodka, cognac, liqueurs. From 90–120 calories per ounce: bourbon, some rums.

To drink and lose weight, you must keep a gimlet (!) eye out for carbohydrate counts as well as calories, of course. An ultrahigh protein diet combined with low-carbohydrate-count drinks can help you shed pounds in weeks instead of months. Minimal carbohydrates are found in gin, vodka, Scotch, and dry wines. Avoid mixed drinks (except those made with low-calorie sodas) and brandy, aperitifs, and liqueurs. Beer is out, too. One exception: A great two-day crash diet allows you hamburger patties (made from lean ground round) and up to three cans of decarbonated beer a day. Especially good for rah-rah girls who still go to beer parties and would like to emerge five pounds thinner.

Basic Diet Rules for Drinking Dieters
1. Check with your doctor.
2. Take vitamin pills.

Not-So-Basic Diet Rules for Drinking Dieters

1. Weigh yourself every day. You should know where you stand, right down to half-ounces. Dieting is fine and drinking is fine—but drinking can make you forget you are on a diet. So check every morning.

2. Try to have a glass of water before every meal. It will make you feel less hungry.

3. Discover artificial sweeteners and low or noncaloric sodas.

4. When you do lose five or ten pounds, reward yourself—with a baked potato (you have earned it) or a new dress or a fur hat. If you opt for food, remember that you are "slipping" just once, until the next big milestone.

5. Sign up for a series of manicures, or get a smashing new hairdo, or try a facial, or better yet all three. Improvement in other directions besides your figure gives you the boost you need to stick to a diet.

6. Don't, don't listen to fatties who will say they don't know why you have to diet. Before you know it, they'll be splitting that fat-making slab of pecan pie with you—the one that makes *them* feel guilty.

Tempting (and Easy) Dinners for Drinking Dieters

Broiled chicken wings basted with teriyaki sauce

Steak tartare

London broil

Broiled beef-kabobs with a few cherry tomatoes, green peppers, small white onions

Omelet with Parmesan cheese

Beef patties with light dab of blue cheese in the center

Broiled brook trout with lemon juice

Steak au poivre

Cold cracked-crab with a mixture of wine and soy sauce (half and half, add touch of ginger)

Scrambled eggs with cottage cheese, chives, and Parmesan cheese

Scrambled eggs with cottage cheese and chipped beef

Scrambled eggs with mushrooms and sherry

Shrimp, hot or cold, with cocktail sauce

Perfect Order-in Lunches for Diet-Drinkers

Hamburger without the roll

Cheeseburger without the roll

Hard-boiled eggs (good with instant-soup powder on them)

Cottage cheese

Keep in Mind

That photograph of yourself in which you are bulging out of your bathing suit.

Caviar has only 35 calories per tablespoon.

You might look fat but you want to feel thin.

A diet isn't self-punishment—it's self-glorification.

Your weight the last time you stepped on the scales.

The clothes you are going to be able to buy.

Love is just around the corner.

Soy sauce can make cottage cheese (or almost anything else) taste better.

Candy isn't dandy; liquor *is* quicker.

Thin girls look rich.

"Stocky," "sturdy," "chubby," and "plump" are just other words for "fat." And a half-size isn't half of anything.

You could look better in bed (without the covers).

Diet Hangups

Men like women who aren't scrawny.

No matter how hard I try I just can't lose weight.

Big-boned girls just naturally weigh more.

Desserts are my downfall.

Calories don't count.

Everyone needs some starch.

Just this once.

No more excuses now. You can drink (be merry) and diet all at the same time. If you get tired of all that good protein, a chilled glass of white wine will pick up your spirits. And, even with all the holidays coming up, nobody at the office parties will know you're dieting (unless you tell them).

Cheers!

CHAPTER 13: LEAVES OF GRASS?

Absolutely no moral judgment intended here, but marijuana is *not* one of the leafy greens to include in your diet. Grass can not only heighten your passions for music and love, but it also does such insane things to your food lust that it ought to stay illegal! Two hours after polishing off a titanic dinner, a few puffs can make you utterly ravenous again! It's not hunger; your relaxed euphoria creates a tingling feeling of emptiness it feels *so* good to fill—and food will taste so extraordinarily delicious! My favorite pot-head told me he gained fifteen pounds in two months—from eating sweets while stoned. *Don't!*

ROD STEIGER. I had to lose thirty pounds after the movie *In the Heat of the Night,* and this is the diet that did it. Breakfast was my biggest meal: two eggs, poached; sausages; black coffee. Then, after an hour, several sets of tennis. Six or seven cold shrimps for lunch. Dinner was cold chicken with crisp lettuce (no dressing). No snacks, no drinks. Hard, yes, but after a week you feel better and begin to sense your body relaxing.

DAVID NIVEN. I won't eat nonsense foods— like cream-cheese dips with potato chips ... you know, all that goopy stuff. I'll eat a man-sized steak, washed down with a glass or two of Bordeaux, but I'll bypass potatoes, much as I love them, for another glass of wine. Solid foods are what I enjoy. They keep me fit and, thank God, at a regular weight.

EARTHA KITT. I ate raw sweet potatoes and clay (that's *dirt*) from the backyard as a cotton-picking kid in North Carolina to kill my stomach pains, and today I still go to the garden for my food. I believe in organic gardening (that's without any poisonous sprays), and when I'm home, I always have one meal (either lunch or dinner) of garden greens. This includes collards, beet tops, and spinach from my backyard. My other main meal will be balanced with either meat or fish. For breakfast: juice and coffee. That's all. So far, so good. No fatty problems.

101

JOAN CRAWFORD. I eat sparingly and often. And I eat slowly. I will not bolt down a bunch of food and stretch my stomach. And I say, "No," when people ask, "Come on, Joan, aren't you going to eat a bit more?"

I like fruit for breakfast, especially that delicious Jamaican fruit called "ugli" (a cross between a tangerine and grapefruit). Or a boiled egg. Midmorning, maybe a piece of cheese. For lunch, a slice of boiled chicken (white meat only), with one or two whole canned tomatoes. (I'm crazy for tomatoes). Dinner's boiled beef or a chop, which I cook with vegetables. No bread ever, nor dessert. Sometimes, I'll make a meal of cole slaw, which is slimming, and I fix a special dressing with dried mixed herbs, lemon juice, Old Monk olive oil (because it's light and pure), and my favorite, Heinz cider vinegar. Yes, I like a cocktail before dinner, and always sip a glass of champagne when I go to bed. It puts me right to sleep.

CLAIRE BLOOM. My diet is simple. I eat a good breakfast—fruit and toast and tea. Luncheon's my big meal—maybe fish or a bit of capon. Dinner's practically nothing—a cup of consommé and a cracker. The less I eat before retiring, the better I maintain my weight.

BARBARA STANWYCK. Coffee's what comes to my rescue. When I have hunger pangs, I brew a pot of coffee—fast. I drink two cups, and I'm all right.

JULIE ANDREWS. I eat slowly, and always try to eat just enough without feeling overfed. This way, I can occasionally have another glass of wine, if I want to, with dinner.

PATTI PAGE. No starches, bread, or sweets. And lots of vigorous exercise.

RICARDO MONTALBAN. I always try to leave something on my plate, never eat everything. But I exercise constantly, lift seventy-pound weights fifty times a day.

BURT BACHARACH. When I want to lose extra pounds, I go on a Chinese-food jag. For both lunch and dinner. Mostly rice with vegetables, which the Chinese undercook. My breakfast is carrot juice, lemon juice, and honey in warm water. In ten days, I'm usually down to par.

KATHARINE ROSS. High protein, lots of fresh vegetables, horseback riding, walking my two sheep dogs. Cakes, pies, chocolates, are *verboten*. When I crave something sweet, I chew on a few raw carrots.

VINCE EDWARDS. Black coffee and fresh fruit for breakfast. I skip lunch, and eat green salad and grilled beef for dinner. If I'm crazy-hungry for pasta, I eat the diet pasta that's made with artichoke flour— only 250 calories a serving.

BOB STACK. If I drink a glass or two of beer instead of a martini or two, I get full—and eat less.

CYD CHARISSE. Three small meals a day, that's how I keep fit. My heaviest meal is lunch. When I want to lose a few pounds, I stick with plain yogurt and high-protein meals. And when I cook meat, I cut off all the fat.

THEODORE BIKEL. I'll drink a glass of wine, but I've cut out hard liquor completely. You'd be surprised at the weight that drops off after a year— once you give up the cocktail routine.

SANDRA DEE. I check the scale daily—and when I'm five pounds overweight, I take drastic action. Juices, lean beef, black coffee.

JIMMY STEWART. Golfing keeps me trim. And simple home-cooked foods like chops and spinach. I'll have a drink, but I'm careful. One or two at the most.

PAULA PRENTISS. I nibble . . . never eat. And I nibble slowly. And besides, I let myself get so hung-up on conversation that the food doesn't matter. Good talk diverts me, and I pick at the food.

DINA MERRILL. I'm convinced tennis keeps my weight down. Skiing, too. But I am careful of fatty foods like whipped cream, butter, and jellies. As a rule, I eat sensibly, even enjoy a cocktail or glass of champagne with dinner.

SHIRLEY TEMPLE BLACK. My husband and I love gourmet foods, but we have our way of compensating for special nights when we dine out on the town. The next day, it's broth and a salad—that's all.

NANCY SINATRA. I'm careful for two or three days, then I'll have something yummy like guacamole. And, of course, when my mother's fixing lasagna, I won't eat all day so that I can have all I want.

MERLE OBERON. I taste foods—if you know what I mean. I'll taste a dessert, but not finish it. Just a forkful or two, and no more. The same's true of rich foods. I'll take a taste, but not eat more than that. I've learned through the years that a taste satisfies me . . . and I don't have to worry then about interminably counting calories.

NATALIE WOOD. I love good food and a cocktail, but when I'm dieting, I munch rabbit foods, like romaine and raw carrots, and stick to such plain main dishes as a piece of boiled chicken or beef. Absolutely no sauces. Or sweets. And in two weeks I lose weight.

ROMY SCHNEIDER. When I want to lose weight quickly, I go mad with really rough exercises and cut out all desserts and starches. In no time I lose five pounds.

ELKE SOMMER. The only snacks I allow myself between meals are a glass of tomato juice or a bite of an apple. I swim, bike-ride, take long walks, sometimes skip rope to work off any extra calories I might have indulged in.

EVA GABOR. I crash-diet with grapefruit, pots of coffee, a teeny steak or bite of chicken, and a lettuce leaf or two. When I really get carried away with Hungarian pastries, I usually go to a health spa for a weekend and let them take over on how I should shed the pounds.

SYLVA KOSCINA. I eat only what I like. I don't force myself to eat what's good for me. If I'm in the mood for a hamburger and apple pie, that's all I'll have. Nothing else. No appetizer or French-fried potatoes. And I always take the bun off a hamburger. I don't like bread, so why should I fill myself with it?

LIZA MINNELLI. I like dieting, because I look forward to the results. I feel as if I have a new image after I lose weight. Just recently, I kissed eight pounds goodbye in a couple of weeks by cutting down on everything. I drank my lunch—usually I mixed a shake in a blender with low-fat milk, honey, berries. Dinner was soup with fresh vegetables and beef bones. Maybe a low-cal soft drink when I was thirsty. That was all. And that did it.

NANCY REAGAN. The Governor and I used to keep fit by riding and swimming; but now most of our outdoor physical activity is curtailed, and while we eat the same good foods, we've cut down on the quantity. We eat half of what we used to eat—and we eat sensibly. Cold cereal, a grapefruit or orange in the morning. Maybe eggs and bacon. Tea with sugar. (The Governor doesn't like coffee.) But our lunch is light. A clear soup, a fruit salad. Possibly a sandwich. Dinner is veal or broiled lamb chops, chicken, or seafood. We've cut way down on breads, sauces, and gravies, although occasionally we have a chicken curry, which we love. The Governor's also wild for macaroni and cheese, and ice cream, and every so often we splurge. We both like fresh strawberries dipped in sour cream and brown sugar, but we never ever eat too much—of anything. And when we dine out at political banquets, we push the mashed potatoes into a far corner of our plates. Oh, yes, one more thing: We like our vegetables plain.

CHAPTER 15: THE DIET ANSWER LADY

Some questions you might have on your mind:

Will all overweight people lose weight if they diet? Yes. Except those very rare few with strange ailments. *Very* rare.

If I lose weight very quickly, will I put it back just as fast? Not unless you go right back to your old gorging routine. There's no proof that a person regains his weight more quickly *just* because he's lost it *fast*. If you retrain your appetite to nutritious and *moderate* eating habits, you should have no problem. Don't abandon control and become an eating machine.

Do you burn more calories in cold weather than warm? No. Climate has nothing to do with your basal metabolism rate. Other things *do* affect it: age (your metabolism rate slows down as you get older); some diseases (the rate increases with fever, thus you can shed extra pounds when sick with the flu); and sex (tragically, a woman's metabolism is generally slower than a man's).

Can I believe the labels on dietetic foods? Yes. Make sure you read them with an eagle eye.

Do vitamins and minerals have calories? No.

I've heard people say that taking vitamin supplements increases your appetite. Is this true? No. That's another Diet Myth.

Is fish really better for a dieter than meat? Yes! A pound of steak can easily contain 2,000 calories (more than your entire daily food allowance), while a pound of fish can have as few as 400.

How often should I weigh myself? It depends. While you're dieting, once a week. (Daily weight loss can fluctuate, and you'll get depressed if you go for three days without seeing the needle drop.) After you've reached your ideal weight, once a day for the rest of your life. Don't skip a single day!

Do you lose more weight by eating six little meals a day than three big ones? Once again, it depends entirely on the calories you consume. Some experts believe it's best to nibble lightly after 6 P.M. because evenings are inactive for most of us and the food just lies in a lump inside you. But ultimately it's burned up—if you've cut down on your total caloric intake. An interesting experiment was done with chickens—one group pecking normally (as chickens do) all day along around the barnyard, another group fed just once a day. The latter, although not any fatter, showed considerably more hardening of the arteries.

What about constipation in dieting? People frequently have fewer and sometimes more difficult bowel movements while dieting because they're consuming less and getting less natural fluid from food. Don't worry, that's not chronic constipation. Drinking a lot of water and eating raw vegetables should take care of things.

Does toast have fewer calories than bread? No.

CHAPTER 16: GETTING YOURSELF DIET-READY

Not that I want to postpone this dieting adventure another minute, mind you (I know that you're all revved up, anxious to start) . . . but take a little time out, now, to put two things in order: your kitchen and your head. It will help if you make some purchases, do some pantry-cleaning, then go over some very subtle—but critical—tips for your new diet mentality.

YOUR DIET ARSENAL

1. A blender—the greatest invention since the wheel. Later on I'll confide the myriad diet miracles this little machine can perform with soups, dressings, drinks. For now I'll tell you this: If I'm going out for dinner at 9:00, and 5:30 finds me limp from hunger, the most filling, simple solution is to toss some low-calorie black-cherry soda into the blender with four ice cubes and a third of a cup of skim milk. Whirl it all up, and out comes this sweet, thick (the crushed ice cubes accomplish that neat trick), cold wonderfulness. Two big glasses worth, for about 35 calories!

If your rich uncle just came through with a legacy, buy a blender with ten speeds. If not, the two-speed (low and high) will work fine, provided it crushes ice.

2. A Teflon frying pan. Butterless frying really works, allowing those otherwise forbidden treats like sunny-side-up eggs, "sautéed" mushrooms, "fried" eggplant.

3. A first-rate scale—preferably just like the one that dear old Doc has in his office. If you can't afford that, either in money or bathroom space, buy the very next best. The machine that must measure your success is not something to economize on. An untrustworthy scale (one that registers 138 pounds at noon and 136 pounds at 12:03 will only incite you to feed your hangups with self-deception. (Remember that "My scale is crazy" routine you've just broken out of?) Well, make sure you have a scale that is boringly sane and reliable.

4. A brand new, fresh array of herbs, spices, seasonings. These goodies make the difference between dreary mealtimes and yippee-what-shall-I-make-for-dinner-tonight excitement. Since spices lose their punch after a few months, my suggestion is to toss all your current ones into the incinerator and start fresh. Go on a shopping spree, experiment with fennel, tarragon, marjoram, dill, cardamom, caraway seeds, all the other pungent exotica you've puzzled over in cookbooks and on grocery shelves but never tried. Remember, herbs and spices are only used in small amounts . . . and last for a long time, making them relatively inexpensive. (Five dollars should buy a shelf-full.) Heretofore undreamed-of variety will revitalize your taste buds. A baked chicken breast with rosemary is—to mix a metaphor—a whole different kettle of fish from chicken cooked in soy sauce and ginger. And the simplest food perks up with the merest herbal touch. (A sliced beefsteak tomato sprinkled with fresh lemon becomes practically princely when you crush basil between your fingers to release the scent, and sprinkle it on top.)

5. A postage scale. No, we don't care how heavy your letters to your mother are, but you'll need the scale to weigh portions of meat and vegetables in ounces. Not every diet calls for this procedure, but calorie-counting dieters have to know the size of their portions just as Weight Watchers do. When you weigh meat or fish uncooked, subtract two ounces for bones and/or shrinkage during cooking. Thus, a raw hamburger weighing eight ounces will eventually provide you with six ounces of beef.

6. Your *Cosmopolitan's Calorie Counter &*

Diet Diary. (It's attached to this book opposite page 128. Tear it out *now*.) You're going to carry it in your pocketbook *everywhere*. What for? So you can write down everything that passes your lips (including calorie counts if your diet calls for them), at least until you get comfortably settled into a diet. That's what for!

7. A new and shamelessly sexy at-home out-fit—one size smaller than your current self. The psychology should be blindingly clear . . . plan to wear it "entertaining" at home about three weeks from now. Hang it up in the front of your closet to remind you, if you happen to be on the verge of forgetting, *why* you're on a diet.

8. Great Supermarket Raid supplies. Before you buy these, clean out the refrigerator and make a care package for your favorite underweight neighbor, containing all boxes of cookies, corn flakes, half-finished cans of peanuts, contents of living-room candy dish, yes, even that rich gourmet cheese you just spent three dollars on and nibble before bed. *Out.* Anything that might seduce you in rough moments must go. If you feel safe having a box of macaroni on the shelf, by all means leave it—you will certainly be eating macaroni and cheese again one of these moons. How many temptations you keep around is a matter of Know Thyself. Are you the type who, in a fit of depression or 3 A.M. sleeplessness, will put on a James Taylor album and whip up half the box of pasta with butter and garlic? (Be honest, *are* you that person?) Then bestow it on your under-nourished friend.

Now for the Great Supermarket Raid. Grab your cart and this basic list:

a. diet soda—a big selection of flavors (The sweet ones are great for low-calorie blender milk shakes; ginger ales and lemons for basting baked apples and peaches.)

b. tomato juice

c. vanilla extract

d. sugar substitutes—liquid and powder

e. vinegar—wine and tarragon

f. instant nonfat dry milk

g. bouillon cubes

h. diet margarine

i. dietetic gelatin, salad dressings, jam

j. fresh: onions, scallions, carrots, cucumber, cauliflower, radishes, tomatoes, green pepper, celery, garlic, sour pickles; lemons, grapefruit, oranges, apples, melon, berries, pears, peaches, pineapple (You won't buy all these at *once* unless you're feeding a family of twelve—but choose from this list.)

k. canned: mushrooms, bean sprouts, asparagus, tomatoes, water-packed tuna, dietetic fruit

l. cottage cheese

m. plain yogurt

n. herbs and spices discussed above

Now, doesn't your pantry look *beautiful?*

YOUR DIET PSYCHE

1. Tell your pals, boss, office cohorts, boy friends, and your Aunt Sadie about your new diet. Why? Their reactions to the revelation will separate friends from enemies. A man who loves you *won't* thrust a bag of hot buttered popcorn at you in a darkened theater; he'll bring you a diet cola, and won't give in to your pleas for a mouthful of his popcorn. As a matter of fact, if he *really* loves you and understands the nature of temptation (you're liable to sit for two hours fixating on that forbidden popcorn, right?), he'll forego the treat himself this one night.

A *real* friend won't invite you over for dinner and produce a casserole of manicotti; won't test your endurance and embarrassment quotient by dishing out pasta to everyone else and boiled chicken to you. She'll serve a cleverly disguised high-protein meal to *all*. A loyal downstairs neighbor you visit often will lay in a supply of sour pickles, carrots, and melon for those evenings you pop in to gossip till 2 A.M. (the hour by which you'd *formerly* have gobbled all the nuts, dried apricots, cheese, and ice cream within reach). Your buddies will also be sure to tell you frequently how terrific you're looking as the needle moves down the scale.

2. Reward thyself. And make the rewards scrumptious, expensive, elegant, extravagant *food*. Remember, you're not going to *forget* food or erase its importance in your life. (That's too much to

expect from anyone!) But the shift will be from sundaes, loaves of French bread, and cream puffs to huge fresh strawberries, jumbo shrimp, and satin-leafed artichokes.

Ideally, your diet should cause you as little suffering and deprivation as possible (because those lead to self-pity, which in turn results in binge eating). And believe me, you don't *have* to suffer! You can be as thrilled when you purchase and devour a mountain of steamed clams, just arrived at your fish store (15 calories each, no butter sauce, thank you) as when you used to scoot home to gorge on a Napoleon. Buy the eighty-nine-cents-a-pound bursting red hothouse tomatoes instead of the pallid three-in-a-carton for thirty-five cents. Splurge on Spanish melon and every other luxury in the market that looks divine— and low calorie. For once, don't worry about the price. Economize on taxis and new lipsticks if you must.

3. Try on clothes often. First, you'll use up your lunch hours in fitting rooms instead of restaurants. Also, if you despise your reflection in that full-length three-way mirror, you'll be inspired. When you *do* start to like the image (it'll be a very short time, you'll see), utter elation will follow!

4. Treat yourself for victory . . . a new record album for every three pounds lost, or that leather vest you've been coveting for ten.

5. Set realistic goals. Don't build expectations bound to leave you feeling you've failed dismally. (Never say, "I *should* lose fifteen pounds in three weeks.") While you're dieting, especially if you've a good deal to lose, visualize the weight in small chunks. Don't think, "My God, I still have eighteen to go" after you've dropped an important seven. Be *positive:* Break down the total goal—say, twenty-five pounds—into lumps of five. You're striving to lose five. Then five more. Bit by bit, the total won't seem monumental or hopeless.

6. The single purpose of your diet is weight loss. If you find yourself slipping into the common fantasy that being thin will also result in (a) the arrival of Prince Charming, (b) a career as an international film star, or (c) the Answer to Life—you'll be nastily

disappointed. The only promise your diet holds is *thinness.* Isn't that *enough?*

7. Keep very busy. Try not to spend a whole Sunday alone in your apartment—just you and the refrigerator. Take this time to catch all those 1930's-movie revivals you've been wanting to see. Or if you're going to spend an evening reading, why not do it at the library instead of lying in bed a mere seventeen yards from tomorrow's lamb chop?

8. Stay out of temptation's devilish path. The gang going out for pizza? You'll meet them *afterward* (but don't you dare feel sorry for yourself). If your next-door neighbor spontaneously invites you for pot luck and you find the pot brimming with beef Stroganoff, feel free to say "No thanks," and come back for after-dinner coffee.

9. Anticipate times when the diet will get rough. And it will. If you've been using food all your life to placate anxiety, anger, and loneliness, you'll very likely have attacks of tension *because* you've lost that caloric crutch. Expect the stormy seas and they won't overwhelm you. The morning you wake up with a depression whose twin is an overpowering urge for sugar doughnuts; the Saturday night he can't see you, so *you* yearn to go see Sam the pizza-parlor proprietor—be *ready* for those moments, *plan* for them. If you've told your co-workers about your diet, they'll be prepared to glare when you reach for a doughnut in the coffee line. Keep your mind stocked with late-evening pizza alternatives: Invite people over for the Late Show, go ice-skating with a friend . . . *anything!*

10. If you slip, no self-hate, recriminations, punishment. The lapse is not critical—*if* you get back on the track tomorrow. Anyway, self-destructive feelings will lead to you-know-what. One warning: Cheating may not manifest itself on the scale right away, so you may think, "Gee, I got away with it. I can do it again." Wrong. The evil truth will show in a few days.

CHAPTER 17: MOVING THOSE LAZY MUSCLES

Notions about dieting—what's good, what's not so good—go through fads and fashions just like attitudes about child rearing. In recent years, exercise for keeping fit has been popular, but exercise for *reducing* has gotten an extremely bad press. Rumor has it that if we roller-skate around the corner for a newspaper, the exertion will so deplete us that we'll ravage the refrigerator as soon as we roll home. The idea, I suppose, is that one's uncontrollable, overpowering appetite lurks dormant, poised to become a voracious demon at the slightest stimulation. That theory, of course, is just so much pot cheese. Appetite, for most of us Fat Souls, is *psychological* (I used to be hungry *all* the time, even when my only activity was dog-earing the pages of a book), and whatever *real* hunger twinges after an hour of field hockey can certainly be quelled by an apple. A five-course banquet just isn't *needed*. As for the unreal hunger (the one in our heads, not our digestive systems), we must deal with it in other ways.

The bad-mouthing of exercise accelerated when nutritionists released figures about how few calories we actually burn through physical exertion. Walking a mile, they claimed, only uses up 80 calories, meaning we'd have to walk forty-four miles (moving briskly, at that) to lose one measly pound; a half hour of strenuous swimming equals one medium-sized chocolate bar, calorie for calorie; an hour of golf only burns 250 calories (no, that's *not* riding in an electric cart!) Upon hearing this news, nonathletic types (people whose idea of vigorous energetics is to forego the remote-control switch for the T.V. set, those for whom bike-riding, tennis, or even hearty walking is torture) gave up in discouragement— or relief.

Some dieters *do* continue to exercise—out of the worst motives! You'll recall that Fat Souls are notorious *self-deluders*, and many of us use exercise to that end. A few years ago, before I knew the facts, I thought an hour of tennis entitled me to eat anything in the world I craved. There was a Chinese restaurant around the corner from the courts where I played weekly. After the workout, my partner (a Thin Soul, naturally) and I would saunter over and without a qualm—we'd just burned up all those *thousands* of calories, you see—put away several orders of egg rolls, some barbecued spareribs, a little chow mein. As far as I was concerned, I was still dieting; I merely felt *entitled* to this *mini-snack* because of all that exercise. Also, since I hadn't the slightest conception how many calories were in an egg roll, I never faced the bad news. Perhaps you've spent a lunch hour running all over town on errands, never pausing, covering two miles with your feet. Then on the way back to the office you stop at a take-out deli, and instead of ordering your usual sandwich and coffee, you splurge a tiny bit on a sandwich *and* a chocolate milk shake *and* a brownie, after all that *hiking*. *There's* self-deception for you!

Exercise is *terrific* and *important* for *everybody* —*especially* dieters. Let's see what it *really* does and doesn't do.

Exercise is the great variable in calorie burning. A sedentary man who sits all day over an adding machine may only use up 2,400 calories a day; an extremely active man, 4,500; a professional athlete, 6,000. If you're naturally more vigorous than sister dieters (that is, your job and life-style keep you on the move), *or* if you take dance classes or ski, you will lose weight faster than they for the obvious reason that you're burning more calories.

What exercise also does is awaken your body (that usually stagnant, overfed lump) and put you in touch with feelings. When exercising, you feel muscles, nerves, and physical sensations that have been asleep too long. This change is wonderful psychologically, since dieting gives you a *new* body that you want to be really tuned in to. You'll be as proud of that body's firmness, litheness, and *shape* as you will be of its *thinness.* I *want* you to be elated—even *cocky*—so your new body will inspire you not to slip back to flabbiness.

Exercise also makes you feel sexier. Yes, it *really* does, in the same way that the *more* you make love, the lustier you feel. Alive and energetic, your physical self *responds.* There's nothing sexier!

Incidentally, the *average* sex act (whatever *that* is) burns about 150 calories. (Now, don't take that as license to follow lovemaking with a sprint to the refrigerator to polish off the cheesecake!)

Completely apart from dieting, exercising is a super means for meeting men: tennis courts, scuba diving classes, the basketball court in the neighborhood school playground—that's where men are. So even if you *hate* all that leaping around, think of the possible results and *keep going!*

What exercise *won't* do is substitute for a low-calorie diet. *No way.* I'm being repetitive, but this truth must be stressed: *The only way to lose weight is to eat less.* Embroider that sentiment on a sampler, and hang it on the refrigerator, or make a tape recording to play while you sleep. Anyway, remember, remember, remember . . . !

Your exercise program can take several forms. Join a modern dance or gymnastics class. (When I studied gymnastics with the leading studio in New York, I was so terrified of climbing the ropes and hanging upside down from the trapeze, I started throwing up in dread before class. I quit after three weeks.) Or you can take, as my friend Vivian does, a rock dancing class that teaches all the new steps and is nifty exercise, too. Yoga is wonderfully *calm* exercise—plenty of rest periods between serene postures that stretch *every* muscle (and it's good for your *head,* too!).

If you're sports-minded, tennis is a superb activity. Even if you're no Billie Jean King—who else *is?*—all that bending to retrieve missed balls is *great* for the abdomen. Bike-riding is not only convenient in large cities, where you are often the fastest-moving vehicle on the street, but also strengthens the thighs and stomach muscles; horseback riding does *not* spread the hips (as rumor had it when I was an impressionable teen-ager), quite the contrary. Swimming (I mean *swimming*, not floating on a rubber raft, reading a magazine and sipping a vodka Collins) is about the *best* exercise there is. Also consider fencing.

If even *reading* these suggestions makes you gasp for breath, if your idea of heavy exercise is trying on and taking off eleven pantsuits at your favorite boutique, how about a little fast walking? Why ride the elevator those four flights when you can climb the steps and firm those thighs? Try walking to work and home, walking to your dentist appointment instead of riding in a cab, taking an hour's walk with your lover after dinner. But the pace must be nippy and brisk to burn calories and be beneficial to the figure . . . and must *not* culminate in a stop at the pizza palace or ice cream parlor.

However you do it, exercise should be *frequent* and *regular*. Sedentary living all year, punctuated by jogging the entire length of Wilshire Boulevard on April 27th, is not where it's at.

CALORIES BURNED THROUGH EXERCISING ONE HOUR

Cross-country skiing	1300
Jogging	600
Swimming (moderate crawl)	600
Dancing (fast)	500
Tennis (singles)	500
Sawing wood	500
Bike-riding (moderate pace)	450
Tennis (doubles)	400
Bowling (very actively)	400
Volleyball	350
Walking (vigorously)	350
Golf	300
Floor-mopping (vigorously)	300

Walking (moderately)	200
Ironing (strenuously)	200
Typewriting	145
Driving	130
Singing	125
Brushing hair	100
Talking on the telephone	50

Like your diet, an exercise program should be personal, idiosyncratic, tailored to *you.* The world's most ingenious gymnastics instructor will *never* get *me* to do gymnastics from a height of more than one inch off the ground, while my friend Bunny swings around the trapezes like a jolly little chimpanzee. Likewise, I certainly wouldn't insist you breast-stroke fifty laps a day when a kiddie's wading pool turns you catatonic with terror.

Following are a carload of exercises. Take your pick. For concentrated spot-reducing, there are exercises for tummy, legs, hips, fanny. Yoga tricks work on special spots, general body tension. There are exercises for allover firming up. And kooky *but effective* activities like belly dancing (ever see an exotic dancer with a pot belly?), dance-ercizes if movement to music seems easier, isometrics to do at your desk, and perhaps zingiest of all—exercises to do with your lover. Hardly seems like work.

Need it be said *once more* that your exercise activities—whatever they are—will never replace the Perfect Diet?

THE FLAT
SEXY STOMACH

If you *have* one, it really doesn't matter what else you *don't* have! Elephant ankles, knock-knees, or forty-inch hips just seem to fade out of sight when your tummy is near-concave. How do you *get* this kind of trim, taut, seductive tummy? It's mainly a matter of exercise, says famed beautiful-body builder Nicholas Kounovsky. (But don't forget: You can't *eat* everything you want and still have a flat stomach—that's final!) Three different sets of abdominal muscles come into play—straight, oblique, transverse—and you must deal with *all* of them if you're to be slim as a snake. Here's a super Kounovsky exercise for each set of muscles:

1. For the straight abdominal muscles: Start from supine position. Sit up, swinging arms forward and jackknifing knees to chest at the same time. (Keep toes pointed, elbows stiff.) You'll feel your tummy muscles tighten as they literally pull you off the floor! Start with two, gradually work up to six.

2. Lie flat on back with one knee bent and arms pointing at ceiling. Sit up (quickly, now, but keep it fluid). Simultaneously, lift legs a few inches off floor and swing arms to the same side as flexed knee. (This twist at the waist helps the oblique stomach muscles.) Alternate sides; work up to six on each.

3. This one's for the transverse muscles. Lie on your back. Start with arms outstretched, one leg pointing straight up in the air, and arms flat on the floor; lower leg sideways and touch your toe to the floor. (The higher your "touch point," the better—aim at your hand.) Do two to six times; switch legs.

LITHE AND LISSOME LEGS

No, cowering beneath a midiskirt *won't* disguise those legs! Don't you want that tissue-weight wool to *cling* to a subtly curved thigh? Shouldn't the knee-to-ankle line that flashes through the slashed skirt be elegantly Dietrich-like? And when you disrobe . . . what then? *Firm* legs have just got to be prettier than floppy ones—and here are the fastest ways we know to get them:

1. *All legs* benefit from this one . . . it tones calves and thighs. Bend knees (go down as far as you can), keeping heels on floor, torso rigid. Then straighten knees, rising up on tiptoe. Do eight times.

2. *Fat legs* need a special regimen of swinging exercises. Swinging is slimming. Only thing is, you must keep toes pointed. Here, the swing is from side to side, but you can also go in a back-to-front direction. Do it to music, fifteen to twenty times.

3. *Thin legs* need bigger, better muscles! Hold on to chairback, with one leg extended behind you. Touch heel to floor —push! Then rise up on toe. Do six times each leg.

4. *Inner thighs* just can't be too firm, can they? Here's a good way to get rid of the flab: Lie on floor, supported by elbow; raise top leg as high as possible, with toe pointed. Bend ankle . . . stretch hard . . . point toe again; lower leg. Roll over on other side and repeat for other leg. Do six times each.

HIP
HAPPINESS

Big can be beautiful ... but not when it comes to hips! Oh, a little soft, voluptuous swelling below the waist is O.K.—*sexy*, in fact—but now we're talking about those protruding saddlebag bulges *no* girl wants! The saddlebags can be carried high or low— just below the curve of your waist or at the top of the thigh. Most hippy girls don't have them in *both* places, but alas, a few unfortunates *do!* If you were *made* that way—yes, it's a hereditary fat-distribution pattern—you know by now that jogging and/or dieting-to-the-brink-of-starvation won't solve the problem. However, there *are* some things you can do to keep the bulges under control while on your Perfect Diet:

SPOT-REDUCING

Exercise expert Lillian Rowen, who works on the torsos of many Beautiful People, says hip spot- reducing is *the* most difficult ... demands constant repetition ... but *can* be done. She advises twenty minutes a day ... predicts results in about two months. Exercise routine must concentrate on the muscle group around hips. (Don't squander energy on your tummy or bosom!) Do exercises with friends—group pressure will keep you at it—and to *lively* music. (The Doors, the Fifth Dimension, the Tijuana Brass, are all good beats.) If your posture is less than perfection, correct it—Miss Rowen says bad posture emphasizes figure faults by accumulating *more* fatty deposits. (Horrors!) Here are two basic Rowen hip-reducing exercises:

1. Lie on side with top leg perpendicular to body. Point toe inward (no ballet turnout), raise leg twenty times. Switch sides.

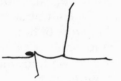

2. Kneel, one knee to chest . . . swing leg back and up fifteen times. Switch legs. Can also be done standing, holding on to chair.

CAMOUFLAGE

Fashion can be your ally (as long as you stay off the beach!) An A-line skirt is the hippy girl's best friend; next-best is a dirndl. Tunics and long jackets are also good cover-ups. Pants? Perhaps—if they're wide-legged. To be avoided like the Hong Kong flu: hip-hugger pants; big, low-slung belts; pleated skirts (especially kilts); clingy fabrics; large plaids and prints. A dark-colored skirt with a light top is an eternal godsend; if in doubt, stick with it. Underwear is getting less and less these days (it may disappear completely!), but girdles *do* still exist. They may not be in, but you *need* them. Don't be tempted by wispy little-nothings—lots of Lycra is for you!

SURGERY

If you are really and truly desperate—and if your hippiness is so extreme as to constitute a near-deformity—consider an operation. Yes, a plastic surgeon can actually cut off all that excess fat! But wait—before you pick up the phone to call the doctor, think again. Reputable plastic surgeons won't *do* it unless you honestly *need* it. *Wanting* is not enough. (One top doctor said: "I wouldn't operate unless the hips were *freakishly* large . . . the treatment can be worse than the disease! Scars are highly unpredictable.") It is not a relatively "simple" procedure like a face-lift, but a major operation involving large amounts of body tissue. In fact, it is an *amputation* . . . and serious complications can follow. There now, we've warned you. If you're *still* interested, talk to your doctor.

THE DELOVELY DERRIERE

Call it what you will—behind, buttocks, fanny, or derriere—what a girl wants is a *beautiful* one! There are scads of exercises for hips, thighs, tummy, and even *ankles*, but the bottom has been sadly neglected, don't you agree? We broached the subject to the experts at New York's Alex & Walter Physical Fitness Studio—about the liveliest place we know for girls to work up a sweat in pursuit of a super shape. "Aha," they said, "you mean the *gluteus maximus* muscles. . . ." (That, it seems, is the name of the big muscles that run diagonally across the buttocks, and they are what largely determine the shape of your derriere.) Here are the exercises Alex & Walter gave us, guaranteed to do absolutely *nothing* but give you a beautiful bottom!

1. Lie on floor on your side, with one arm propping up head. Keeping legs straight, touch floor behind you with toes; then make an arc in the air and touch toes to floor in front of you. Do four to six times on each side. Don't stop breathing! Walter says that's what creates tension.

2. Hold back of chair for support and bend over, keeping arms and legs straight. Raise leg to the side, *with heel turned out*. (A ballet turnout's wrong here—it exercises the thighs, not the buttocks.) Do three to four times on each side. "If you feel a cramp," warns Alex, "stop."

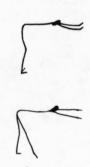

3. With one hand on hip, hold chair and lift leg to the side, again keeping heel turned out. Body must remain straight; don't bend at the waist. Do four to six times and switch sides. Try a double kick, without touching floor (three to four times), if you can take it . . . but don't overdo!

ISOMETRICS AT YOUR DESK

The isometric technique can be applied to just about *any* part of your body that needs work. And there's none of that exhaustion in leotards while flopping about on the floor—you can do *these* exercises at your desk! It works this way: You build tension for six seconds in each muscle group (see the details following), then relax. Repeat three times. Voilà!

1. GRACEFUL POSTURE

Place fingers at base of neck. Point chin toward ceiling. Try to make elbows touch behind your back. You'll feel pressure in neck and shoulders. Marvelous for relieving midafternoon head-aches and general tension.

2. FIRM THIGHS

Stand erect (your best posture, please) with a telephone directory between your feet. By pushing your heels against the book, trying to bring them together, you'll feel tension in your thigh muscles.

129

3. SENSUOUS SHOULDERS

Place your fist in the palm of the other hand. Try to push your fist through your palm. You'll feel the stress in your shoulders. Hold for six seconds, then relax. Repeat exercise the usual three times.

4. CURVY BACKSIDE

Stand in doorway with left knee against frame. Place hands on frame at chest level. Push with knee and hands as if you were Samson destroying the temple. Feel the tension in your backside. Repeat with right knee.

5. TIGHT TUMMY

Isn't that where a good figure begins? While sitting, lean forward and place hands firmly under your calves. Then press *down* with your hands, and at the same time, push *up* with your toes until you feel stress in the abdomen and waist.

6. FIRMER BUST

Make a steeple with your fingertips, spreading the fingers as far apart as you can. Press fingertips against each other as you simultaneously try to make your shoulders touch beneath your chin. You'll *feel* the tension that tones up pectoral muscles supporting your bosom.

7. PRETTY ARMS AND NECK

Rest your head on your desk as though you were tired. Place your hands on the edge of the desk. Now push down as hard as you can toward your knees with both fingers and forehead. You'll feel stress in your arms and neck. Particularly *good* for correcting a flabby jawline.

ALL-OVER
BODY FIRMING

O.K., it's not just a question of behind-the-knee fat-roll or backside bulge—your whole body is one big problem! Good, you are an honest girl, and here is a super-exercise-plan just for you.

The name of this particular regimen is Weight Training—a combination of several movements using five-pound dumbbells (which cost about ten dollars at sport shops)—and it emphatically *won't* make you muscular. The first group of exercises (1 through 6), for limbering up, must be followed immediately by the second (7 through 14), which are the real figure reshapers. Start with the minimum number. The exercises should be done three times a week, or twice at the least. *Warning:* If you suspect the slightest thing wrong with your heart or spine, see a doctor before starting the program.

1. ELBOW CIRCLING

Start: feet apart, arms sideways at shoulder-level, elbows bent, hands touching neck. Movement: Describe large circles with elbows—forward, upward, and back. Breathing: *in* as elbows move forward, *out* moving back. Repetitions: ten to twenty.

2. SIDE BENDS

Start: feet apart, arms stretched sideways at shoulder level. Movement: Raise right arm as you bend trunk to left. Reach down on outside of left thigh with left arm. Then repeat, raising left arm and bending to right. Breathing: freely. Repetitions: ten to twenty each side.

3. KNEE RAISING

Start: feet together and hands on hips. Movement: Raise knees high on the chest, moving each leg in turn. Breathing: freely. Repetitions: ten to twenty each leg.

4. TRUNK ROTATING

Start: feet wide apart, arms stretched sideways at shoulder-level. Movement: Rotate trunk, arms, and shoulders, looking behind. Rotate to opposite side, legs, feet, and hips remaining still. Breathing: freely. Do only once.

5. ANKLE TOUCHING

Start: feet and arms as in Exercise 1. Movement: Bend to left, reaching for left ankle with both hands; return to starting position. Repeat, bending to right. Breathing: *out* on way down, *in* on way up. Do only once.

6. FEET APART JUMPING

Start: feet together, arms at sides. Movement: Jump astride on toes, raising arms sideways to shoulder-level; jump back to starting position. Breathing: freely. Repetitions: ten to twenty.

7. PULLS

Start: feet a few inches apart between two dumbbells (which should be placed pointing from front to back), knees bent to right angles, back flat (not hunched), face forward. Movement: Reach high with the head, grasp dumbbell in each hand, come up on toes as dumbbells reach shoulder-level. At this point elbows should be pointing downward. Breathing: *in* on way up, *out* on way down. Repetitions: eight, progressing to twenty or thirty. Purpose: Stimulates breathing and raises the pulse; exercises legs, back, arms, and shoulders.

8. SIDE BENDS

Start: feet wide apart, toes pointing sideways, a dumbbell in one hand, free hand resting on hip. Movement: Bend freely from side to side. Breathing: freely throughout. Repetitions: ten with dumbbell in right hand, ten in left; progressing to twenty or thirty each hand. Purpose: Trims the waistline, mobilizes spine.

9. KNEE BENDS

Start: heels together and raised, toes turned outward, dumbbell held in each hand at hips. Movement: Keeping trunk vertical, bend knees sideways until you are in little more than a half-squat. To maintain balance at first, place a book under heels. Breathing: *out* going down, *in* coming up. Repetitions: ten, progressing to twenty or thirty. Purpose: Exercises legs and hips, heart and lungs.

10. WAIST SWINGS

Start: feet wide apart, toes pointing sideways, both hands grasping globes of one dumbbell, both arms straight and stretched to one side at chin level, shoulders turned in direction of arms. Movement: Swing dumbbell in half-circle downward, passing knees on its way to the other side of the body to complete a half-circle. Gradually turn shoulders in direction of the swing, bending knees on the downward movement and straightening them on the upswing. Breathing: *out* on downswing, *in* coming up. Repetitions: ten, progressing to fifteen or twenty. Purpose: Exercises hips, waist, and legs.

11. PULL OVERS, KNEE BENDING

Start: Lie on back, legs straight
and together on floor, arms
stretched overhead at floor-
level, a dumbbell in each hand.
Movement: Bring both knees
onto chest while raising dumbbells until arms are perpendicular to trunk at shoulders.
Lower arms and legs to starting
position. Breathing: *out* as you
raise knees, *in* as you lower
them. Repetitions: ten, progressing to twenty. Purpose:
Exercises the shoulders,
tummy, and bust.

12. SEESAW PRESS

Start: feet apart, toes pointing
sideways, elbows bent and
pointing downward,dumbbells
held at shoulder-level. Movement: Reach up high with left
dumbbell, straightening arm,
while bending trunk to right.
As you start to lower dumbbell,
bend to other side and press
right dumbbell overhead. Breathing: freely throughout. Repetitions: eight each side, progressing to fifteen. Purpose: Exercises arms and shoulders, spinal
muscles, and waistline.

13. TRUNK CURLS

Start: feet astride, toes pointing
sideways, arms straight down in
front of trunk, both hands
grasping globes of one dumbbell. Movement: Turn shoulders

to left and bend downward to touch left foot with dumbbell, rounding spine slowly and gradually straightening spine on return to an upright position. Repeat, turning shoulders and bending down to the right. Breathing: *out* on way down, *in* coming up. Repetitions: ten to fifteen times each side. Purpose: Exercises back of thighs, hips, and spine; stimulates breathing, raises pulse.

14. ARM CIRCLING
(Seen from above)

Start: lie on back with legs straight and apart, and a large book under your shoulders, arms straight and crossed at the wrists over lower abdomen, a dumbbell in each hand. Movement: Raise dumbbells up and toward opposite shoulders until arms become uncrossed as they pass face. Then continue backward and over head, gradually completing a circle with each arm and arriving, eventually in starting position. Breathing: *in* as dumbbells start to shoulders, *out* as they return to starting position. Repetitions: ten, progressing to twenty. Purpose: Exercises shoulders and bust.

BASIC YOGA TO START YOUR MOTOR HUMMING

It's not just your body that's hefty . . . remember that Fat Soul? Yoga can help, and you can do it! Naturally, you don't believe that, because you've seen Yoga pictures before, and those girls were all standing on their heads or convoluted like paper clips. Well, the girls in those pictures were doing *advanced* Yoga. *These* instructions are for the very simplest, nursery-school-level, Basic Beginner's Yoga. (No, you don't have to stand on your head!) TV's Richard Hittleman has done more to popularize Yoga than anybody, so an instructor from his New York Yoga for Health School explained these easy postures for a novice. Afterward you'll feel terrific . . . relaxed, stretched-out, no creaks or kinks or aches or tension—and with more energy than when you began! That, of course, is the secret of Yoga—and why so many busy, famous, beautiful people do it.

Perhaps you're a baby lounge-lizard, and never do anything more strenuous than file your nails. Try these simple Yoga postures. (Slow . . . easy . . . yes, *breathe*.) After a few weeks your body and your *spirit* will feel happier and healthier. *Then*, if you want to try standing on your head or playing pretzel, you can buy a Yoga book and take it from here. And if you don't want to progress? Mr. Hittleman says: "There's nothing wrong with staying a beginner forever . . . the benefits to your body and spirit are exactly the same!"

138

1. SIMPLE TWIST

Almost like a visit to the chiropractor for unkinking your
spine! (Back trouble? This will
help.) Sit as shown, then slowly
turn head and twist body as far
to the left as possible. Relax.
Switch sides.

2. KNEE AND THIGH STRETCH

A great inner-thigh firmer.
Sit and place soles of feet
together, close to body. Clasp
hands around feet, pull them up
very gently. (Get knees close to
floor.) Relax; repeat.

3. SIDE RAISE

Firms muscle tone from the
waist down: legs, thighs, hips,
buttocks. Lie as shown; push
down hard with right hand,
while raising legs from floor.
Keep legs together and in line
with body. Relax; repeat;
switch sides.

4. CHEST EXPANSION

Develops bust, slims upper arms,
improves posture, increases
blood supply to brain. (Can't
hurt, can it?) Clasp hands behind back, straighten arms. Bend
backward from your waist
without forcing. Hold for a few
seconds, then bring arms—
hands still clasped—up over
back, and simultaneously bend

forward from the waist as far as
possible. Relax your neck . . . let
head flop over . . . hold for
several seconds. (Don't bend
knees!) Straighten up slowly,
unclasp hands, relax, and
repeat once more.

5. COBRA

Great for getting rid of tension
and stiffness in the back and
neck. (That's where tension
"trigger points" are located.)
Side effects: firmer arms,
buttocks, bust. Start prone,
with elbows bent and hands
pointing inward. *Slowly* arch
spine and raise trunk off
floor—push with hands, tilt
head back—until arms are
straight. (Don't strain; keep
elbows bent a bit if you can't
straighten them easily.) Lower
trunk to floor . . . relax . . . repeat
once more.

6. ARM AND LEG STRETCH

A marvelous way to develop
balance and release tension.
(Lousy sense of balance? Do it
leaning against a wall. You see,
there's no such thing as *cheating*
in Yoga!) Raise arm high over
head. Now slowly bend the
opposite leg and pull foot up
toward your back. Relax;
repeat on the other side.

7. HALF-LOTUS

This posture is a tranquilizer. Do it when you're depressed or upset; it will quiet the emotions. (Also good for flabby thighs if *they're* depressing you!) Place left foot against right thigh. Now place right foot on *top* of left thigh. Rest hands on knees, thumb and first finger in a circle. (Yes, it *matters!*) Relax in position, hold as long as comfortable. Stretch legs, massage knees, then reverse legs.

MORE YOGA FOR
THE WORKING GIRL

Your problem is probably not so much needing another exercise plan as needing the willpower to stay *with* one. Working girl's Yoga just may be the one you *can* stay with. Marcia Moore and Mark Douglas (Mr. and Mrs. Douglas), authors of the book *Diet, Sex and Yoga,* have developed a simple exercise plan that you can follow every day with "no trouble and no exertion." Yoga, they say, will make you feel like a new girl and look like a body beautiful—within reason.

Start with the six basic exercises. They're easy to learn and, once mastered, will come naturally. You'll have to do them every day—for a while. Once you're in shape, you'll only have to do them two or three times a week. The routine gets easier as you go along, and the exercises only have to be done once or twice daily, if you're lazy. Then, instead of building up the number of times you do each exercise, you can combine exercises and spend less time getting the same results. Or, if you find (horrors!) you enjoy exercising, you may want to *add* variations to your regular routine. No hair-tearing scenes of guilt if you miss a day or two—or even seven. Just pick up where you left off.

Ready? Here's the exercise plan.

YOUR BASIC ROUTINE

1. THE ROCK AND ROLL

a. Lie on your back on a
carpet, folded blanket, or thin
mat. (Don't make it *too* soft or it
won't work.) Bend your spine
and raise your knees, lifting
your feet from the floor. Clasp
the back of your knees with
your hands. Raise your head
toward your knees and slowly
rock back and forth on your
curved spine, letting your feet
leave the floor as you rock.
Isn't that fun? You've been told
all your life to stand up straight
and now you're slouching on
purpose, and it's *good* for you.
At first, you'll only do jerky little
"rocks." As you loosen up, try
longer rocks. Soon you'll be able
to sit with your knees up to
your chest, feet flat on floor, and
rock all the way back until your
toes touch the floor behind your
head. (You should see Marcia
Moore do this one. She turns
complete circles like a wheel.)

b. When you're really a pro—
in a week or two!—you might
want to try this exercise from a
sitting position with legs crossed.
Bend your head forward until it
comes as close to the floor as
you can get it—but don't bump
it! Rock back on your curved
spine, clasping your toes, until
they touch the floor behind your
head. Keep the rock going a
few times. Wheee!

2. THE PUMP

Stay flat on your back. Raise
your right leg *slowly* while
breathing in. Lower your leg and
breathe out. Do the same with
your left leg. Try this at least
five times. *Don't* hurry. Do it as
slowly as you can. Now try both
legs *together.* Raise and
s-t-r-e-t-c-h your legs luxuri-
ously—as much as you can
without bending your knees.
Hold. Now, you may find that one
of your legs is shaking. Don't
get upset—that means you're
doing the exercise right. See if
you can concentrate on that one
leg and the muscles that are
working hard. See if, just by your
concentration, you can stop
that leg from trembling and
still hold the position. Try the
exercise one more time. It's
good for your back, tummy, and
legs. It'll help your posture, too.

3. THE HINGE

While flat on your back, raise
your legs (knees straight) to an
angle of forty-five degrees.
Once again, concentrate on the
trembling (or working) muscles.
Hold this position for . . .

4. THE RUSTY HINGE

Stay flat on your back. Raise
your legs, knees straight, until
your thighs are just a shade off
the floor. Hold it. Feel what it
does to your abdomen.

5. THE SWIVEL SLIMMER

Lie on your back. Stretch your
arms out at a forty-five degree
angle, keeping your palms flat on
the floor. Breathe in, raising
both legs until your heels are a
few inches off the floor. Keep
knees straight and together.
Swing legs to the right as far as
you can. Let your hips roll,
until your left leg is above the
right. Back up to center position.
Lower legs slowly to floor,
breathing out. Repeat, swinging
legs to left side. The Swivel
Slimmer is great for the waist.
Do it at least twice to each side.

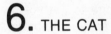

6. THE CAT

This is a sensuous exercise that
is good for your upper arms and
back. Get down on your hands
and knees. Be a table—keep
your back parallel to the floor,
thighs and arms perpendicular
to it. Turn hands in until fingers
are just touching. Breathe in,
bend elbows, and lower chest to
floor, or as close as you can
get it. Your derriere will be up in
the air; your neck will touch
your fingers; the small of your
back will curve in, like a cat's.
Now purr a little while a few
seconds go by. Reverse procedure to straighten up (and
that includes breathing *out*)
slowly.

      When you can do the Cat
easily, try this variation.
Assume original table position,
breathe in, raise head as high as

you can. Extend right leg in back
of you with knee straight. Hold
it until you feel pressure in
your back. Breathe out while
slowly going back to the
starting position. Repeat with
left leg. Another variation: Still
kneeling in the original position,
pull your right knee in and up
under your body toward your
chest. Try to touch your knee to
your forehead. You're now
stretching your back in the
opposite direction. You probably
won't be able to touch your
forehead the first few times—
the important thing is to *try*.
Now do it with the other leg.

This is your basic daily Yoga routine to get you in
shape. It really isn't hard, is it? As you improve,
you'll find it takes almost no time at all—about ten
or fifteen minutes for all six exercises, once you've
learned them. The most important thing to remember
is never, never *rush*. Everything should be slow and
easy. You can't pull any muscles or hurt yourself if
you take your time and move leisurely.

Eventually, the six basic exercises aren't going
to be enough of a challenge for your supple body.
Here are two exercises to substitute or add to your
daily routine:

7. THE INVERTED POSTURE

Lie flat on your back, breathe in,
raise legs together—heels
together, knees straight—until
your hips are off the floor.
Use arms, palms flat on floor, to
help lift yourself up. Support
lower back with hands—palms
on buttocks and thumbs hooked
on top of your pelvic bone
with fingers around waist

pointing to small of back. (This
position sounds ridiculously
hard, but you'll find that you'll
assume it naturally—it's the
only way you can hold yourself
up.) Tilt legs back over your
head, curving your whole body.
Hold this position as long as
you can without moving. Now
slowly return to starting position,
breathing out. (You may feel
that you have to jerk your legs,
with your knees bent, to get up to
the correct position in the
beginning. But soon you should
be able to do a snaky all-in-one
fluid motion to get your legs up.
Work on it!)

8. THE SHOULDERSTAND

This is a senior Inverted Posture,
where your entire body is
vertical, supported by your
hands. Your body is straight,
chin against your chest. Say
good-bye to the tummy that is
staring you in the face. Hold the
inverted position as long as
you can. If you find yourself
swaying, shift legs slightly in
toward your face. Return to
flat-on-back position . . . slowly
curving spine toward floor.
This exercise can replace any
or all of the others if you don't
have much time. You can do just
this one and work on most of
your body all at once. But *do not*
try the Shoulderstand until you
have mastered the basic six
exercises listed above.

Along with a sensible diet, and you know what *that* is, these simple exercises will make you a happier, healthier girl—vital and sexy, brimming with energy. *Everything* wakes up—your organs, muscles, circulation—you start *using* and discovering your whole self. You actually discover what you were blessed with at *birth*—a strong, healthy body that can do just about anything you want it to do.

If you want to go farther with this plan, and you probably *will,* get a copy from your bookstore of *Diet, Sex and Yoga,* by Marcia Moore and Mark Douglas ($6.95, published by Arcane Publications, York Cliffs, Maine. Or you can write directly to Marcia Moore, c/o Yoga, York, Maine. She also runs a Yoga Information Center for people all over the United States.) The book even tells you how to stand on your head. You may find yourself upside down for ten minutes a day while you read, talk on the phone, or just contemplate the wonderful new body you're living in!

MY FIGURE'S FINE . . .
BUT MY *NERVES!*

Tense? Jittery? Taut as a cat burglar? Well, join the rest of us! Tension, you know, is an occupational hazard for a girl with a job—unless perhaps you're working as a milkmaid or a mattress tester or something. And if you're on a diet as you should be, you've *added* reasons to be uptight: Your longtime tension-dissolver, *food* (especially *fattening* food) has been taken away! Because tension shows in your face, your posture, and your disposition, it needs taking care of. You do it with exercises—a special *relaxing* kind. Here are some to do at home or at the office on hellish days. You'll feel tension just *oozing* away!

1. CAT-BACK STRETCH

Straightens out the spine and smooths all those knots in back and shoulder muscles. (That's where tension tightness is concentrated, and that's why you get a headache and stiff neck from it!) Start by getting down on all fours, with knees slightly apart. Arch your back for a few seconds, then hump over, curving spine the *other* way. Now pull backward (don't shift hands or knees) until you're sitting on your heels. Relax . . . feel all the nasty tension just flow out of you! Repeat as many times as you wish.

2. RHYTHMIC ROLLING

Soothing . . . and stretches all those bunched-up back muscles. Clasp hands under drawn-up knees. Rock forward (head down), then backward, now forward again. Keep steady rhythm; don't do it *too* vigorously or you'll bump your face with your knees! Rock ten to twenty times.

3. THE FLOP-BOUNCE

Legs apart, flop over from waist; let arms just dangle. Bob over each foot a few times, then straighten up, swinging arms in a giant circle.

4. TWO EXERCISES TO DO AT YOUR DESK
(Instead of screaming!)

When your neck and shoulder muscles tighten up, even *typing* seems a strain! Sitting erect at desk, entwine your fingers with hands resting in lap. Lower head until you feel a pull in the neck muscles. Raise arms—elbows straight—till perpendicular to ceiling. Stretch all the way up from the base of your spine. Hold for count of five.

Here's another way to get the knots out of your neck: Rest hands on knees. Hunch up your shoulders so they almost cover your ears. Hold for a count of three, then push your shoulders down as hard as you can, elongating your neck at the same time. Now relax, drop your head, close eyes. Swing head slowly from side to side, dipping it down at center-swing, pulling it up at each side of arc. You should feel neck muscles stretching on each upswing.

5. RESTING POSITIONS

These two positions are relaxing and tension-releasing; you can rest in them as long as you like . . . maybe even doze off! Each should be very comfortable, so you must make little adjustments until you find *your* "best" spot. (You may want to bend your knees or elbows a bit in the first position; in the second, you may keep your knees six inches apart—or twelve inches—it's up to you.) When you find your optimum position, relax completely, close your eyes, let your mind go blank. The second position also gives relief from menstrual cramps!)

BELLY DANCING SHAPE-UP FOR THE INHIBITED

Have you ever *seen* a belly dancer? Shalimar, who performs at the Egyptian Gardens café on New York's West Side, is not, as you might expect, a hirsute, hippy extra out of an old Near Eastern movie epic . . . she's beautiful! Her undulating body is taut, limber, her lines smooth and flowing—not a bunched muscle anywhere! In addition to this great body, Shalimar seems to emanate a beautiful spirit, a sensual mystique that surges around her as she moves.

If you want to improve your figure *and* soak up that special sexy magnetism she and her belly-dancing generate, take some lessons from Shalimar. Here are the basics; try them to music (*Port Said,* Mohammed El-Bakkar, Audio-Fidelity Records, ASFD-5833; *Sultan of Bagdad,* Mohammed El-Bakkar, Audio-Fidelity Records, ASFD-5834; *Turkish Delight,* Gus Vali, Musicor Records MS-3092).

1. BASIC WALK

The introductory step of belly dancing. It's a quick, provocative "pitter-patter." You begin by stepping flat on the right foot, then tap the floor with the ball of your left foot. Then step flat on

left foot, tap with right. As you
walk, twist your body from side to
side. Knees are slightly bent,
and arms wave gracefully in the
air as you move. "End each
step with a bump," says
Shalimar. "*Click* your hip. . . ."

2. HIP BUMP

"Don't overintellectualize," says
Shalimar. "Stop thinking . . .
just move . . . swing . . . feel
sexy . . . it should be in your
flesh." Twist sensuously; torso
muscles pull taut as you move.
Marvelous for your waist!

3. BODY ROLL

The real "soul" of belly dancing.
You sort of crouch down, arch
your back, and then suck your
stomach in. Rising from the
crouch, you let your stomach
push *out.* Arms also profit from
this number. You raise them as
you rise. The slowness of the
motion puts tension in the
upper arm, which, it's hoped, will
firm it up.

4. UPPER TORSO ROLL

"Another great waist cincher,"
says Shalimar. "You do *eight* of
these." Start by bending
forward, then rolling to the
left, to the back, to the right.
Just let your head *hang.* "This
is good for midriff bulge, too,"
Shalimar adds.

5. BODY WHIP

A backbreaker, but terrific for the waist and torso. Lie on the floor with your legs folded under you, and do exactly the same Torso Roll you did standing up. (It's harder now that you're lying down.) Shalimar does it quickly, letting her hair swirl after her. Lying on the floor, it seems, and rubbing against its hard surface is a wonderful way to break up fat.

6. COBRA CRAWL

An undulating, inchworm motion. Raise your shoulders, then your diaphragm, and drag body along the floor, using heels for leverage. It looks terribly sexy (when done *correctly*) and slims the entire body. (Did you ever see a fat cobra?) You're supposed to imagine that you *are* a snake— a pretty one—and keep your undulations slow and graceful. (The slower you do it, the more tension is produced in your body, and the more muscle tone improves.)

7. PELVIC ROLL

The most important step of all. Push your fanny to the left, then stick it out in back as far as it will go, then to the right. Pull your pelvis up and start again. When you do it *right*, movement becomes fluid and circular. Rotate your pelvis with abandon . . . muscles and bones will begin to act like well-oiled machinery. You'll actually feel sexy. The spirit of belly dancing will at last enter your creaky system.

DEBBIE DRAKE'S DANCE-ERCIZES

No, you don't have to go as far as Saudi Arabia to find a dance that works figure magic. America's exercise sweetheart Debbie Drake developed this jazzy dance routine to trim you in Occidental style. Follow the step-by-step instructions to zippy music in four-quarter time; put them together in sequence and you're practically ready to appear in an MGM musical!

1. WARM-UP WIGGLE

Stretch left arm toward ceiling, right arm down. Lean to left side, bend left knee. Bounce your left knee four times, keeping the right knee straight.
    Now stretch right arm toward ceiling, bend right knee and bounce four times. Repeat this exercise, bouncing left and right knees once again.

2. SMOOTH THIGHS

Bend left knee and place left hand on left thigh. Swing right arm forward, making counter-

clockwise circle four times.
Bounce knee simultaneously.
Bend right knee, and exercise
with left arm and knee. Repeat.

3. LUSCIOUS LEGS

Hands out at sides. Put weight
on left leg and swivel right knee
in, using the ball of right foot.
Repeat four times. Now reverse,
putting weight on right leg.
Then repeat entire exercise.

4. SUPPLE SHOULDERS

Bring right shoulder forward,
then up to ear, then backward
and down—making circle. Do
four times. Reverse to left
shoulder and repeat four times.
 Bring both shoulders
forward at once in circular
motion. Repeat four times. Now
repeat all three shoulder
exercises.

5. TERRIFIC TUMMIES

Feet apart, bend forward and
touch floor four times with
fingertips.
 Stand erect, bend those
knees, lean backward, and snap
your fingers four times briskly.
Still leaning backward, place
hands in relaxed position
behind your back. Bounce four
times. Then do last three
exercises once again.

6. DISAPPEARING WAISTS

Lean toward left, bending left knee. Stretch hands toward ceiling.

Then bring arms down in pendulum motion for seven beats—nearly touching the floor. On count of eight, lean toward right, bending right knee, and reverse. Repeat exercise again . . . then back to the Warm-Up Wiggle. Repeat all six exercises until record stops . . . then relax!

JOGGING

"If you can't run a mile in twelve minutes, you're in very poor shape!" This pronunciamento comes from Kenneth Cooper, M.D., Major, USAF, author of the best seller *Aerobics* and originator of the whole jogging-for-exercise craze. His statement may throw you into either a depression or a tantrum. Why would any girl want to run a mile in twelve minutes? (What girl—Dame Margot Fonteyn aside—could?) Well, you might want to for several reasons. The main one is that *men* are doing it. They're setting their alarms for 5:45 A.M. and jogging before breakfast. They're skipping lunch to jog. They're foregoing Napoleon-brandy nightcaps for a pre-bedtime jog. Wouldn't it be rather fun if he asked you to join him? ("Once around the park, and then home"— that kind of thing.) Besides being with him, what else will jogging do for you? Plenty—because, unlike isometric or calisthenic exercises that build up only the skeletal muscles, aerobic exercise can do lovely things for your whole body, even where it doesn't show. The key to all this goodness is oxygen. Your body needs oxygen to produce energy, and the more oxygen you can get flowing through your bloodstream, the healthier you'll be. The best exercise, then, is one that demands a lot of oxygen and conditions your body to deliver it. (If your chest heaves and your lungs almost explode after a frantic dash for the bus, your body isn't capable of delivering the oxygen when you really need it—and that kind of challenge is what separates the fit from the unfit!)

It may take a few weeks to get into the jogging routine and build up your wind and endurance; once you do, you'll start feeling the improvements that Major Cooper calls the "training effect." Your lungs will be able to process more air with less effort; your heart will be stronger and will pump more blood with each beat. (A well-conditioned heart may save itself as many as thirty thousand beats per day!) Blood vessels will be bigger and better. Muscle tone and internal organs benefit, too, and so does your figure. Though you may not lose weight, you'll turn fat weight into lean weight, drop inches from your waistline, firm up your legs, stomach, and upper arms. You'll eat, digest, eliminate, and sleep better, too! (And it *might* even improve your disposition. . . .)

Is jogging the only aerobic exercise you can do? No, but according to Major Cooper, it's the best. Others—almost as good—are swimming, bicycling, walking, and running in place. Tennis is O.K., too, provided you're a lousy player. (If you're *good*, you don't have to run around enough to get all the benefits.)

All the men we know who have taken up jogging are crazy about it, so maybe you will be, too. But don't start getting any ideas about entering the Boston Marathon next year—it's for men only.

SWIMNASTICS

New, fun, easy . . . swimnastics are simple little exercises that get your figure in swimsuit shape while you're *in* the swimsuit. Do them in waist- to chest-high water: The density creates just enough resistance to exercise and tone your muscles, but not enough to strain or stiffen them. Swimnastics were created by YWCA-instructor Elizabeth Richardson Charles and have been taken up by body-conscious people all over the country. You have to do *something* in a swimming pool . . . why not perfect the figure? Water should be around eighty degrees—just right for relaxing the body and pulling out tensions. Beauty of it all—you stay cool as a seal while you exercise. Start off your daily swimnastics by simply bouncing up and down in the water. Shake yourself after each exercise. This is your guarantee against aching or strained muscles.

1. GIANT STEP

A super way to stretch and beautify thighs and calves. Proceed in three steps. First bring one knee to your chest. Clasp it with your arms. Next extend the leg straight out. Now take a giant step with the outstretched leg and repeat the procedure with the other leg. Continue the giant steps all the way across the pool and back again.

2. LITTLE RUNS

Easy to do, great for toning your whole body. Trip back and forth across the pool, keeping your arms above water.

3. LEAPS

Take long leaps from one leg to the other across the pool. A top-notch way to slenderize legs, hips, even ankles.

4. ARABESQUES

Stretch and elongate the torso. Hold on to the side of the pool, lift one leg back as far as you can, keep your leg straight, stretch and hold. Alternate legs ten times.

5. WAIST BENDS

Leaning from one side to the other, and forward and back-ward, will take inches off your waistline. For a longer stretch let your head go into the water. Do five bends each way.

6. FLUTTER KICK

Another excellent exercise for slimming calves, upper legs, hips. Hold on to the pool side, bring legs almost to water level, and flutter-kick rapidly *under water*. Do two or three minutes a day.

162

SHAPE UP WITH SOMEONE YOU LOVE

It's *much* more fun to work out with a man. (Husband? Lover? Special friend?) Here: a group of great exercises you can do with the loved one of your choice.

1. PUSH-UPS FOR TWO

He lies flat, supporting your weight on his raised arms. Hold it for three seconds; then he slowly lowers you, bending his elbows till they touch the floor. Make yourself light: Tense your muscles, keep hips up and back straight. Do four to six times. This one's great for his chest and biceps.

2. HOLD-DOWNS

For your thighs, waist, tummy. Lie flat on your back, hands under head, arms touching floor. (*His* job: to make sure they stay there!) With legs angled to one side, lift top leg up and down a few times. Keep knees straight.

Now, try to bring legs together in midair. Angle legs to other side and repeat. Next, your turn to hold *him* down.

3. BACK LIFTS

This one's a challenge! Stand back to back, arms locked. As he bends over, you're lifted right off the floor. (Fit your hips into the small of his back or it won't work.) Slowly scissor your legs in the air. (You'll know when to stop!) As he straightens up, you return to the ground. This is great for *his* legs, back; your *all*.

4. SPREAD-EAGLE SEESAW

(You did it in kindergarten, remember?) Hold hands, keep arms straight, and rock slowly back and forth. Go over as far as you can in both directions, but try to keep knees straight as you pull each other. Do it four to six times.

5. BOUNCE BENDS

Bend over from the waist, facing each other, and put your hands on each other's shoulders. (Really *stretch* your arms and back.) Now, bounce slowly up and down about three times. If you keep your legs straight and your back just slightly arched, you'll feel the pull all down your legs. The lower you bounce, the better.

6. BACK-TO-BACKS

Sitting back to back with hands
clasped, stretch arms up, relax;
stretch again till you feel loose
and limber. Then . . . as he slowly
doubles over, you're pulled up
off the floor. (He takes your
weight on his shoulders.) Next,
he gently lowers you back to
sitting position. Keep feet in
place the whole time. Do
three to six times.

KILLER EXERCISES

Now, there's just one tiny catch (rarely mentioned) about exercises, and that is: The ones that really *do* something for your figure are tough, grueling, strenuous *monsters!* (Not to put down gentler exercise—indeed wonderful, and will accomplish much in the way of suppleness, poise, posture, tension-releasing, flab-firming, and so forth . . . but *won't* usually make you a whole size smaller!) Novices are not usually in good enough shape to do killer exercises correctly . . . don't have the stamina. So the trick is to work up to them gradually—which may take six months or a year. Now we've warned you of the painful reality—but if you're a relentless conqueror like Princess Luciana Pignatelli, Jackie Onassis, Pat Lawford (all killer-exercise practitioners), you'll learn to do them regularly and never even get very much out of breath. (And they will—honestly—really *do* it for your shape; you'll burn off over 200 calories in ten minutes!) Here are some to tackle (worked out for us by the Alex & Walter Physical Fitness Studio), each directed at a vital anatomical area. Needless to add, don't even *attempt* these monsters if you're a cowardly cream puff or if you have any physical ailment, like a trick back!

1. HIPS

Kneel, elbows straight, and shoulder-neck area relaxed. (*Don't* arch back.) Extend one leg to side (knee straight!) and kick upward four times. Now, keeping leg extended on same level, sit back slowly on opposite heel. Return to kneeling position. Repeat three times. Leg *still* extended to side, kick forward—toward head—four times. Now collapse for a minute; then repeat the whole series with your *other* leg! If you're a real tiger, you can do eight kicks instead of four. Supergirls can support their weight on one arm only.

2. BUTTOCKS

Using a piece of furniture as a barre, bring knee to chest, then extend leg behind you, as high as possible. Bounce leg upward twice. Repeat eight times. Leg still extended, do four knee bends . . . then four toe rises with supporting leg. (In ballet terms: *plié* and *relevé*.) Repeat entire series with other leg. Keep extended leg straight and lifted high as you can, toe pointed throughout entire routine.

3. THIGHS

Lie on floor with legs wide apart, hips raised off floor, weight supported on arms. (If your arms and shoulders aren't up to the task, you *can* do this with hips touching floor, but results won't be as good. The higher your buttocks, the harder it is to do—and the more effective.) Cross one leg over the other, arching it as high as possible, and bounce toe on floor twice. Now swing it back to original position, bounce toe twice. Alternate legs.

4. STOMACH

Sit-ups really *are* the very best cure for a bulging tummy—it'll flatten out in no time! Hook feet under piece of heavy furniture for anchorage—legs apart—and clasp hands behind head. Starting from supine position, raise upper torso to sitting position (try to come up in one *fluid* motion) and touch elbows to knees. Head should lead; back *must* be rounded as you sit up . . . otherwise, possible back strain! Exhale as you come up; inhale as you lie back down. Do four times to start, work up to more. Twisting torso to touch elbow on opposite knee makes it *harder,* so try when you feel ready for greater challenge!

5. RELAX
(After your Herculean labors!)

Your muscles have been pumping away like little well-oiled pistons. Give them a good soothing *stretch* to prevent tension knots. Bend knees so that soles of feet are together; hunch over—holding toes—and bounce up and down in a floppy, no-strain way, head and neck

168

totally relaxed, spine curved.
Rest elbows against inner
thighs, forearms on calves.
(As you bounce down, arms
press legs closer to floor.) There,
now! Get up, feeling all smug
and virtuous . . . it's not *every*
girl who has the talent and will
power for killer exercise!

CHAPTER 18: HOW TO LIVE IN THE WORLD

While you're on this dieting trip, it would indeed be super if you could remove yourself from your day-to-day world. If only you were rich or free enough to retreat temporarily from *all* the hunger-making traumas and hot-dog wagons lying in ambush. But that temptation-free Shangri-La probably doesn't *exist* (I'm sure there's a Carvel stand in the New Guinea jungles by this time!) Anyway, you have your job, social life, family—all part of the Real World, and *they* can mess up your diet unless you learn to handle them *right now!* You'll need *will power* and a never-flagging talent for shaking your head from side to side. Here's how to tackle the following Big Bad World situations.

DATES. If he's a loving, steady man, he probably won't hassle you. There is hardly a restaurant where *you* can't find broiled fish or chicken, an omelet, or plain roast beef, while *he* shovels in his potato pancakes with sour cream to his cholesterol's content. (And as I've said before, if he truly *adores* you, he may forego them completely so as not to drive you mad with envy and greed.) But perhaps he's a blind date, or a first- or second-timer, and for some reason you don't want him to know you're dieting. If he says, "I know the cutest little taco joint," you absolutely do not have to agree. Tell him you've been there and found a roach in your guacamole. Tell him you'd rather never eat again than look at a taco. Or pretend you're violently allergic to whatever diet doom he's suggesting.

Now, if he's a poor struggling actor and a Blimpy hero sandwich is all he can afford, insist on going Dutch (that tenet *is* part of the Women's Revolution, you know), or subtly invite him to your place for dinner, or suggest that somewhere in town there must be a chop suey hole where you can munch vegetable chow mein. If none of these ploys diverts him from the junk-food route, either tell him you're trying to lose weight (I think you should *always* tell, anyway) or drop him. (Think how many replacements a svelter you will lure!)

About inviting a man for dinner: If he's new, you really want to impress him with the extravagance of your culinary genius and with the massive efforts you've expended just to feed *him*. To whip up a dinner marvel that meets those requirements—and is also low-calorie—will take all your inventiveness, but it can be done. You *could* make a divine noodle pudding (to accompany meat and vegetables), but pass it by yourself. If it's a noodle pudding of *genius*, he'll be so busy stuffing himself that he'll undoubtedly never notice you're abstaining. The difficulty with *that* tactic is that you'll be *dying* to eat it after all that fussing to *create* it. Why not fuss instead on a rare roast beef, perfect spinach salad with bits of bacon and crumbled hard-boiled egg, a vegetable casserole, and (for *his* starch treat) *one* simple baked potato with sour cream. If he brings wine, have a glass. If you're buying it, make sure it's rosé or dry white.

What love-nibbles to keep in the house for your steady man (assuming he's a skinny who needn't repent for *your* sins)? Well, what can you keep around without eating it yourself? If the presence of a pint of ice cream in your freezer means that you will not be able to focus on anything else until it's been eaten, then out with it. If lover needs some coffee crunch while watching the Late Show from bed, ask *him* to bring it, and throw away the leftover crumbs. Same with nuts, cookies, or whatever else strikes his

Thin Soul fancy. By all means stock up on chunky peanut butter for him—*if* you're not aroused by peanut butter. We're only worried about your tender spots, your vulnerabilities. A dieting friend of mine is a reformed cheese freak, and refuses to keep it in the house. If guests drop over for cocktails at the last minute, she has to run out—perhaps in curlers and no face—to pick up some wine cheddar and crackers. But she prefers that sprint to the daily temptation of having cheese *right there.*

COCKTAIL PARTIES. For me, this All-American institution is the deadliest seduction of all. To begin with, you're generally a bit tense, so the pull toward pacifying hors d'oeuvres or a relaxing Scotch and water is overwhelming. Then, too, everybody *else* is drinking—can you stand around with empty hands? The *rare* cocktail party host thinks to have diet Pepsi at the bar, and you *know* what's in those appetizers: at a chintzy party, potato chips and sour cream dip; an elegant one, Camembert, Swedish meatballs, and great wedges of fresh pumpernickel. An elegant fête may also sport maids who appear every five minutes with sterling silver trays of irresistible exotic hot tidbits. (They're so *little*, why not just a *taste*?) Oh, the *terrors* of the cocktail party! Here's how to minimize the dangers:

1. Have a glass of milk or an orange right before the party, so you'll be less hungry.

2. Drink *something.* If there's no diet soda, ask for tomato juice with lemon and lots of ice. If there's none of *that*, club soda with a squeeze of lime, or with the merest *nip* of Scotch for taste.

3. Position yourself at the *opposite* end of the room from the food. I know all too well what happens when you're cheek-by-jowl with the smoked-salmon-on-toast platter: A heated flirtation with a groovy man develops, you're slightly nervous . . . and that hand reflexively darts toward the food-comfy . . . once, twice, *again* . . . you don't even *notice* you're doing it! Paradoxically, the nervous eating *doesn't* relieve the tension one teeny bit.

4. Concentrate on conversation, seeing old friends, meeting new men . . . *drag* them into intimate corners, away from the *food!*

BUSINESS LUNCHES. Read *The Expense Account Diet: How to Lose Weight on $24.95 a Day and Master the Rules of the Lunch Business* (by Jonathan Dolger, Random House, $3.95). Its funny-but-serious premise is that if you are dieting, like to drink, and must expense-account lunch as part of your business life, you can enjoy low-calorie haute cuisine.

For you, privileged being, no cottage cheese and canned fruit cocktail, no hamburger patty dozing on wilted lettuce. Tycoon that you are, you order the saumon fumé (30 calories a slice), an endive and dandelion-green salad (75 calories), and a glass of the driest champagne (90 calories). Or a dozen Malapeque oysters (160 calories), artichoke vinaigrette (75), and a cup of fresh raspberries (70 calories). How about Beluga caviar, at ten dollars per (but minimal calories), with a smidgeon of gazpacho or a heart of palm?

Mr. Dolger lists endless restaurant exotica: hot leeks in dill sauce, cold trout carpione, water chestnuts with baby shrimp, mousse of ham with kumquats . . . all divine, all expensive, all *fine* for dieters. The only limit to your choices is the tolerance of the company bookkeeper.

Business lunches have growing power in the urban work world. Sometimes actual *business* is even discussed, real deals made. At those times, drinking becomes a vital part of the encounter. I frequently have lunch with editors to discuss past, present, or future projects. And I always order a drink. Why? Because psychologically it creates a mood of comradery, even though both parties may be hustling each other. I order a virgin Mary on the rocks, which is a bloody Mary (tomato juice, spices) *sans* vodka. Nobody ever pokes fun—mostly they don't even notice what I've ordered (so concentrated are they on the anticipation of their own first martini of the day); and if they *do* query, "What on earth is *that?*" I either explain that I'm dieting or say that having a real drink during the day puts me instantaneously to sleep (which is indeed true). My sipping a "drink" puts my partner at his ease; in case he wants to order several, *I* order several, and he doesn't feel guilty or angry for guzzling alone.

If you have a choice of restaurants for a business lunch, select Chinese, Japanese, or Polynesian—but close your eyes to tempura or fried wonton, focus on vegetables, raw fish. Luckily you won't be lured by desserts in those Oriental palaces.

Places to avoid: French restaurants offer death-dealing sauces, German ones grotesque portions and fattening sausages. (You *can*, however, stuff yourself on sauerkraut.) Often the fancier French and Italian restaurants arrogantly *refuse* to serve plain broiled something without the cream or wine sauce. Try telling the difficult waiter that you are fiercely allergic to butter and if that fillet of sole arrives with so much as a thimbleful, you're liable to go into the *most* embarrassing set of convulsions his restaurant has ever witnessed. You'll get what you want. Be firm. Do not become intimidated. If your luncheon desire is a triple shrimp cocktail, or a double order of fresh asparagus and a glass of white wine (and if your diet calls for this), do not let a waiter's fish-eye whip you into submission.

YOUR VERY OWN KITCHEN. Hopefully, we've *already* minimized the Lure of the Looming Refrigerator. It's stocked with items you *can* eat, void of dangerous foods. Still, for many people its humming *presence* threatens. Eating four cans of water-packed tuna and five peaches over the course of a Sunday spent in bed with a cold is not exactly superb dieting.

If you work at home, the refrigerator is an even bigger problem. I suggest that for the period of your diet you work elsewhere. Borrow a friend's apartment (you're much less apt to rape *her* pantry), rent a cheap office, work at the library if possible.

For nights at home, make sure you have plenty of time-consuming, hand-occupying chores—not just television-staring leisure. It's very difficult to eat while you're sewing a new shower curtain, almost impossible *not* to if you're lying on the couch listening to the new Kris Kristofferson album.

YOUR FAMILY. Are Friday nights reserved for dinner with Momma? Sunday afternoons? Does she spend, like mine, two days preparing the feast for her returning "kinder"? Is *all* the food—be it

Jewish, Italian, Greek, or WASP—starch and dessert? How do you let her know you're slenderizing without throwing her into agonies of anguish over your health?

How you let her know is, you let her know. Kindly, sympathetically, maturely, but *firmly*. Just because you want her to prepare chopped steak and string beans instead of spaghetti or blintzes does *not* mean you are rejecting her—*you* know that, but must make it clear to *her*. Food is *not* love, it's only food. Even if your mother is too set in her ways to learn realistic nutrition, *you* need no longer fall into the family caloric trap. Point out to Mother that if she is really on your side, she'll want a svelte daughter, not a hefty, heart-condition-prone one. Yes, I *know* that's easier said than accomplished—but try!

You'll have to fight your *own* old habits, too. Regression to baby eating compulsions the minute you arrive at your family's doorstep is a very common and difficult hurdle. That environment probably taught you bad eating patterns; what's more, perhaps with your family you feel anxious, angry, or unloved. The instant Patti arrives at her folks', tension drives her to nonstop eating till she leaves. When she was dieting, she developed two family-visit rules. One, she stopped going to the weekly food fest (gave work excuses) until she was well on the road to thindom and could afford a lapse. And even then, she arrived one hour after dinner (with a white lie ready) just in time for the fruit-cake-and-coffee scene, but too late for mashed potatoes and gravy.

SKI/BEACH WEEKENDS. Have you ever noticed the shocking amount of food consumed on communal-living weekends? Skiers say the strenuousness of their sport makes food a vital feature of ski weekends, but I've noticed the same degree of gluttony in shared beach-houses, where the occupants' most vigorous exercise is applying suntan lotion to legs. Food is *social*—for most people. *You* must find *other* group pleasures for the duration of your diet.

If you're doing the group's shopping, you unfortunately must consider the skinnies' needs, and will indeed have to load up the wagon with Sara Lees, bacon, four kinds of rolls, stacks of sliced salami. If you can bear up under those temptations, try to get the shopping duty—at least *you'll* remember to buy some dietetic gelatin and plain yogurt. Your only consolation for two days of watching everybody else eat constantly: The main courses in group houses usually consist of swiftly prepared and gobbled steaks and hamburgers rather than irresistible gourmet concoctions that simmer alluringly for *hours*.

Do try to stay away from the house as much as possible. Ski weekends are easier—out on the slopes all day. (And how many of those ski-lodge greasy hamburgers can you polish off anyhow?) However, be extra wary of drinking *après-ski*—those hot grogs can beckon powerfully when you're frozen and exhausted. (If you *must*, try tea or coffee with the *tiniest* nip of cognac.) At least don't turn a small lapse into disaster by binging *and* guzzling.

If there's one other person in the house who's dieting, try sitting next to him/her at all meals.

VACATIONS. Dieter's nightmare: You've spent a minor *fortune* on a seventeen-day excursion to Italy, and once in the land of one of the world's great *hautes cuisines*, you're expected to live on braised celery? A week's needed rest in St. Croix, nothing to do but pamper yourself with sun, blue water, romance, but *skip* the coconut daiquiris? How about checking in at one of those sixty-dollar-a-day hotels (all ambrosial meals included), ringing for room service, and the waiter wheels in a silver-covered tray bearing . . . skim milk and a soda cracker?

I personally believe it's nearly *impossible* to diet on vacation. Let's be realistic: Vacation means self-indulgence; dieting means self-sacrifice. The two simply don't blend. But there are a few measures you can take:

1. Postpone your vacation. Shouldn't you go when you're nice and thin, anyway, so you can shop for exotic new clothes, feel glorious in a bikini, attract elegant strangers? If you then gain a couple of pounds, they won't be catastrophic (as they might be midstream in your diet).

2. Forget the diet completely. Splurge, gorge, enjoy. Accept the Big Price to be paid afterward. But how will you feel when you get home to discover you've regained every single pound you worked so hard to lose? Consider the pros and cons *very* carefully—you know your temperament best.

3. Try some compromises. When I go to St. Thomas, my favorite vacation haunt, I decide beforehand that I'm willing to gain five pounds or so. (Now, I *could* gain fifteen with no effort at all.) I make the choice either to diet strenuously but drink (I adore pineapple-coconut daiquiris—about 250 calories apiece) or vice versa. I do one or the other, *never* both. (That would be a fifteen-pounder.) The semi-indulgence keeps me from feeling *too* deprived; but it's not nearly so destructive as it *could* be. Another compromise might be skipping one meal a day. (I'd think even omitting breakfast would be allowable on short vacations.)

CHAPTER 19: THE PLATEAU

Everybody *talks* about dieting plateaus, but you never believe they will happen to *you*. Here you've been plugging along, happily losing two or so pounds a week, watching your mirror-image shrink before your very eyes. You're sticking to that Perfect Diet, and everything's proceeding well. Then one sunny Wednesday morning you arise, hop onto the scale (Wednesday is the day you've chosen to do that— naked, before breakfast), and the needle hasn't *moved* since last week. Why, just yesterday you were taken to lunch at the snazziest bistro in town, closed your eyes to the rum cake on that obscene pastry wagon, drank black espresso instead. Where's your reward for all that goodness? *Why me?* you scream silently to the scale. Angry, sullen, and hopeless, you're just liable to run out and wolf down an order of pancakes and sausage (don't forget the butter and maple syrup) just for spite.

Don't let this situation sneak up on you. *Expect* the plateau. It will happen, definitely. And if you are going to diet for, say, three months, the plateau may occur three times. It is your body's mechanism for countering all the changes that have been taking place (from the lessened intake of calories) so its vital processes aren't messed up. In other words, your body is taking a rest from the vigorous effort of burning its stored fat. Your body's water balance readjusts itself. The basal metabolism rate may even drop, temporarily making it *harder* to burn more fat. But cheer up. Even without a poundage loss, fat is being redistributed. One morning you may awake to find yourself the owner of a gloriously flat belly, although the scale registers the same as yesterday.

The danger weeks, according to one nutritionist, are the third, sixth, and ninth, but the pattern totally depends on individual idiosyncracies. Another doctor says a plateau can last as long as two weeks. Obviously, there are no rules. *Do* anticipate the plateau, and go merrily on with your diet, knowing that the next week, or the week after that, your virtue will be rewarded.

PART THREE

KEEPING THIN FOREVER— YES, REALLY!

CHAPTER 20: WHY IS IT A PROBLEM?

You're *there!* Gloriously, deliciously, sexily, happily thin! Whether it was a seven-pound skirmish or a full-fledged fifty-pound Battle of the Bulge, you've made it. On the one hand, you feel a miracle has happened . . . you look in the mirror and see a body you really like—*yours;* on the other hand, you know miraculousness had zero to do with it. Every vanished ounce took good old Protestant Ethic hard work. Proud, aren't you, and full of self-love, excitement, ecstatic vanity? Good! Many pats on the back are in order.

You know positively that you'll never gain back those pounds. Good heavens, it's too much fun trying on those wee sizes, buying terrific outfits in far-out colors, when just a short time ago you thought only of fashions to *hide* your shape. *Now* all you want to do is show off your figure, parade, be whistled at. Walking alone across a crowded room is a kick instead of the old nightmare. You wouldn't step off this new golden road you're on for anything in the world, right?

You'll *never* understand those case histories you've read about people who regain all the weight they've lost, pound for pound. *That* relapse obviously will never happen to you; not an ounce of lost flesh will find its way back to your body beautiful.

Since the name of this game is Realism, let's talk realistically about maintaining your gorgeous new frame. I'm going to begin by telling you that keeping thin will be a *problem*. Yes!

Everyone who struggles through a diet to arrive at a new figure is utterly certain she's safe. Being thin is so great—why would anybody backslide? Logical enough, yet the statistics don't lie: More than seventy-five percent of dieters who reach their ideal weight regain every lost pound within two years. (For crash-dieting pill poppers, the awful number is ninety-nine percent!) It's a pity, but it's true. And if you're addicted to diet books and magazine articles, you know they rarely talk about this painful subject. Maintaining weight loss looms as the most arduous and unsuccessful part of dieting. Whether the surplus is eight or eighty pounds, the hangups are the same.

Why? a skinny new you asks incredulously. Well, to begin with, you've lost the incentives and gratifications once provided by actual dieting. The healthy, spartan self-discipline, the feeling that *you* controlled your destiny (*and* your body), fed your growing self-esteem. Shopping for clothes two sizes tinier, the heady sensation of a once-tight dress now baggy, the awed compliments of friends, the needle on the scale plunging farther and farther downward—those rewards encouraged you. You went to a party and saw somebody you'd been out of touch with for a year. "My *God*, how fabulous you look!" said he. "You're so *thin!*" You touched a place on your body that used to be chunky, and not a centimeter of loose flesh jiggled.

After the novelty wears off—and alas it does—*most* of the external prizes also disappear. Your man begins to take the new you a little for granted, no longer licks his chops every time your silhouette crosses his line of vision. And you, too, become accustomed to a new size and shape. Now you have only *interior* motivations, which must bravely survive the loss of encouraging back-pats and verbal lollipops.

Surely we're not virginal enough to believe that all those years of bad eating have been wiped from the great psychological ledger in the sky! In your head, there's still a residue of cravings, anxieties, depressions that caused your weight problem in the first place. After more than three years for me, I still want to reach for ice cream the instant life gets rough. The truth is, we Fat Souls are never really cured—a key fact to remember. Like former smokers and drinkers, we face danger *every day*. For us, the risk is even worse! We *must* eat, can't decide to give up food forever.

Every overweight person somewhere deep inside cherishes the fantasy that once she finally achieves thinhood, her entire life will change.... job performance or love life will improve, or Federico Fellini will spot her at the airport and decide she's star material.

Perhaps the fantasy is not so dramatic: "I'll *like* myself," or "No one will ever reject me again." Although drastic physical changes obviously do transform people who've lost *scores* of pounds, psychiatrists say even *their* self-images (*inside*) unfortunately alter very little. They still *think* of themselves as obese, despite the mirror's truth, and continue to despise themselves.

For those of us who don't have *mountains* to shed, even the *external* changes probably aren't extraordinary. The quality and quantity of my love life stayed relatively constant before and after dieting: Men who weren't attracted to me when I was chubby were not necessarily panting for *thin* me—tough but true. My career hassles, too, did not vanish with the pounds. And I have not yet found the Holy Grail.

Whatever post-diet changes occur in *your* life, they'll probably be less extravagant than the expectations, and if you're not careful, disappointment at the chasm between fantasy and reality can easily lead to masochistic eating relapses, weight regain, further self-punishing binges, more weight, guilt and self-recrimination, more weight, and so on . . . a familiar cycle in the annals of fatness.

The relapse statistics for crash dieters are, repeat, really dispiriting (which is why I've been stressing *non*crash programs). The psychology is easy to understand: Crashers lose a lot very fast—yippee!—but then what? They still don't know any more about food and dieting than they did before, haven't begun the de-brainwashing process of changing their bad habits. I've seen friends fresh from a scorching three-week blitz regime on which they've dropped a big fifteen pounds—and the very next day they're back to coconut cream pie. Right then I make a small mental bet with myself: How many weeks till the fifteen reappear? Three? Four?

An even more graphic example: The obese daughter of a famous movie star, who longed to lose weight fast, had surgery to close her stomach so that all the food she ate traveled directly to her small intestine, and calories didn't accumulate. After she lost a heap, they reopened her stomach—and *you* know what happened, right? She gained back every single pound.

Another common daydream is that once you are thin, you will have completely lost your urges for everything but broiled flounder. Would that this were the slightest bit true. Habits indeed do change, yes, but fattening food is, let's face it, simply divine. And always will be. The discovery that you'll have to deny, deprive, and discipline yourself in certain ways for the rest of your life can be motive enough to drive formerly-fat you right to the cookie factory—so beware!

Another *après*-diet problem: general laxness. When you're dieting, if you slip one day or get dragged against your will to a pasta party, you're always *acutely* aware of what and how much you're stuffing into your mouth. So the next day, back on the diet track—the slipup wasn't catastrophic. But how about when you're not dieting any longer? How do you resume normal eating? And—the primary question— *what's normal eating?* Is it normal to polish off two helpings of spaghetti and meatballs, a piece of garlic bread, salad, and two glasses of Chianti? Or is that a mini-binge, cause to go back on the diet tomorrow?

If your Perfect Diet isn't rigorous, you may stop posing these questions to yourself, and just continue the joy of eating. Many diet experts state that once you reach your perfect weight, you can eat everything you wish. What they never mention:

"Eating everything you wish" is not synonymous with eating *everything*. There *are* those of us who, given *that* sentence to live by, would devour all that wasn't nailed down.

If you looked at dieting as a *temporary* respite from a regular eating pattern to be returned to from a safe position of thinness, you're in heavy trouble. You'll never again be able to eat the way you did before—not the same kinds of foods, in same quantities, or with the same frequency—unless you want to *look* the way you did before.

CHAPTER 21: HOW TO MAINTAIN A SVELTE YOU

Just as you found your Perfect Diet, geared to your individual tastes, delights, and needs, now you'll want to decide on your Perfect Maintenance Plan— a life-style to keep you deliciously thin forever, allow you to relish the fattening wonders of the world without paying the awful price of overweight. You don't have to be on a *diet* for the rest of your life, certainly needn't pretend the words "malted" and "apple turnover" don't exist. On the other hand, you must treat yourself like a reformed smoker or alcoholic: In the eating department, you are frail, vulnerable, liable to attacks from the past. And you must remain on guard for your whole life. Ominous? Well, I certainly don't mean that *one* to-hell-and-back crazy chocolate orgy means absolute cataclysm. Far from it. But you and I, as Fat Souls, foodaholics, are *never* immune to the virus of overeating. And we want to be among the small percentage of strugglers who do indeed stay thin.

You've new weaponry for the battle. First, you've really educated yourself about eating and could practically write a Ph.D. thesis called "Calories: Myths and Realities." You know that steak is fattening, asparagus ambrosia. You've learned hints for staying full, content, well fed, while also mastering your head, how it makes you eat, what it makes you crave.

189

Then, too, you've changed some of those bad habits—now you're substituting an apple for a cupcake, nibbling strawberries instead of jelly beans. Never again will it be possible for *you* to add five pounds to your frame by carelessly eating three between-meal fruit yogurts a day under the delusion they're low-calorie.

You've also learned never to eat unless you're *hungry*. The need to consume the leftover spaghetti because—as the man said about Mt. Everest—"it's there" no longer haunts you. *Some* economies aren't worth it! Standing around the coffee wagon munching a doughnut and chewing the fat is crazy: Are you *really* hungry, or just being sociable and careless? That habit is finished too, right?

You've also trained yourself to exercise more—perhaps by frequent bike-riding, or a modern-dance class, or a fifteen-minute early-bird session of stomach tighteners. Maybe, like my cousin Dennis, you've conditioned yourself to climb the five flights of stairs to your apartment every night, and can't even remember what the elevator operator looks like.

The single most important rule for keeping fat *off* is: Weigh yourself every day. During your diet, you did this once a *week* to prevent obsessiveness and gloom in case the needle stayed stationary for a few days. Now—*and for the rest of your life*—you must weight yourself with the same *daily* ritualism as brushing your teeth or taking the pill. Every morning. Naked. Here's why: It's so easy for pounds to creep back, you won't believe it. The first time I went to California, for two weeks, I had no scale, didn't really think I was eating much (and rationalized away doubts by thinking how activity just *burned* away extra calories). When I came home, I had gained six pounds! If I'd had a scale with me (now I always manage to find one if I'm going someplace for more than a week), I wouldn't have allowed the excess to go beyond two.

If you wake up one cheery morning and discover something new has been added to the scale—namely a pound on *you*—that's the day to diet. As you know, I'm not a believer in crash programs for long-term dieting. But I'm a great devotee of the one-or-two-day blitz to restore your body to its ideal self. (Chapter 23 contains a selection of crashes for post-Christmas, pre-bikini, the day after the night before, all those times when a couple of pounds have sneaked on and you want to make them scurry away before they become a *cause célèbre*.) After all, nobody expects you to be perfect, never to slip or slide.

How do you find out what's normal for you, what you can indulge in and what you can't, what will hold your present weight and what will catapult it skyward? Tough question, mostly because the answer is—like dieting itself—an individual matter. Trial and error is one way. If you've been eating reasonably and ungluttonously, yet have gained a pound—well, you're doing something wrong . . . perhaps drinking a bit more than you realize, or indulging in heavy nighttime nibbling while reading in bed. *Examine thyself.* Go back to writing everything down in your diet diary for a week, or return to calorie counting to ferret out the mistake.

Why not consider making your diet—the one that made you thin—your whole life-style? By that I mean, if you love the Weight Watchers regimen, why not try to *live* on it, just going off for special occasions? (We *do* assume you won't try to live forever on a crash diet that omits basic nutrients! Check with your doctor before making any diet a way of life.) And, of course, since you're not trying to lose but just *stabilize,* you *can* eat that big Italian dinner one night, or have an ice cream soda after the movies, or go to a bagels 'n' lox brunch, always returning to the diet the next day. (Need I mention that the ice cream mustn't be every day, that you can't have it *and* popcorn *and* chocolate while watching the flick?)

Once thin, you've nothing but your judgment to rely on. The simplicity of dieting (you can't have candy, and that's that) is gone. Now you *can* have candy—but when and how much? You've a new freedom, and freedom can be scary. It may also turn into anarchy.

Here are two more maintenance styles to consider. One girl I know keeps her new state of slenderhood (two and a half years old) by dieting strictly from Monday morning until Saturday morning, on 1,000 calories a day. (She's a mathematician and *relishes* all that computing.) Saturday and Sunday she eats *anything* she wants—I do mean anything. I've seen her pack away a Saturday afternoon shopping lunch that astonishes even me. Her weekends are no-holds-barred pampering. But she has found, through all kinds of trials and mistakes, that this method works for her. Remember—she's absolutely strict and faithful to her diet for five days, never relapses; so the one and a half pounds she puts on over the weekend come off. (Incidentally, even though you may feel like you're regaining six pounds on a weekend food orgy, doctors say it's hardly possible to put on more than one and a half pounds in two days.) If that life-style sounds appealing, here are the details:

THE LOW WILLPOWER, HIGH-PROTEIN DIET *(that allows for binges and slide-backs).* Dieting is a *bore*. Only a nondrinking ascetic can continue on that nonfat, nonsugary, low-carbohydrate, lettuce-y stuff forever. Eating is one of life's most primitive and satisfying joys. Eating is sexy (how about that love feast in *Tom Jones*), but you want to *look* sexy too and this requires not eating too *much* . . . probably counting calories. How to reconcile the two: the urge to indulge and the wish to stay slim? Who has the willpower to stay on a diet indefinitely and never cheat? The high-protein, low willpower diet allows you to go to hell on weekends, provided you shape up in between. This diet is a lifetime one designed to keep off the weight you've so painfully and bravely shed. (If you haven't *already* done so, you must avoid the weekend binges and slide-backs, and use only the Monday-through-Friday part of this plan *all seven days.* By doing this you should be able to lose approximately three pounds per week. *Then*, when you are down to your desired weight, you're ready to binge on the weekends and stay slim.)

Yes, you may have two glorious days of eating and drinking every Saturday and Sunday . . . anything you want . . . lap it up, swill it down, smear jelly on it. Say yes to all the sinful offers! The damage is just about zero if you follow the Plan: Atone for your wantonness with Guilty Monday, a day on which you eat sparingly while exercising considerably; and then Tuesday through Friday eat sensibly but happily on 1,000 calories per day. Comes the weekend . . . another binge if you like.

How can such a plan keep your figure in shape? Most figure-conscious people think that a weekend of self-indulgence adds five or six pounds of bulge.

It isn't true! Dr. Allan L. Blackman, an internist in private practice on Manhattan's East Side who specializes in weight control, tells us that you will rarely add more than a pound and a half to the body on one weekend no matter how much you've eaten or *what* it consisted of. Every Monday morning Dr. Blackman has a crowd of penitent reducing patients in his office who *think* they've gone way round the bend with their eating and done irreparable damage. "I *know* I've gained ten pounds this weekend," a conscience-stricken dieter will wail. "There was this party Saturday night and another one Sunday and— well, I don't know what came *over* me." Dragging herself to the scales, she's amazed to discover she's *lost* a pound and a half since the Monday before. (The doctor's patients usually check in once a week.) "That's because she stayed on a 1,000-calorie-per-day diet from Monday to Friday," Dr. Blackman explains. "If she had stayed on the diet seven days, she perhaps would have lost three pounds. The point to remember is that it's the over-all weekly calorie count that matters. You can put on an extra pound and a half over a weekend and *take it off* by the next Friday night." Dr. Blackman should know—this is how he keeps his own weight constant.

Over eight years ago he reduced by eighty pounds and *hasn't put it back on.* He's a nondrinker— which helps—but he eats what he likes every weekend. "I believe humans were designed to yield to temptation!" the doctor says. "But using this plan I've never felt better."

You too should be able to follow the Weekend Binge, Guilty Monday, Sensible Tuesday-Through-Friday Diet Plan and find that you've plenty of vitality during the week, look absolutely first-rate by the weekend. Try it and see.

The Weekday 1,000 Calorie High-Protein Diet. Monday to Friday are the high-protein, shovel-it-in days when you build up energy and vitality. (Dr. Blackman designed this diet for the young woman with a full-time job that demands a lot of sitting (and unfortunately produces a lot of spreading).) It allows for 1,000 calories per day. If you do much running around, you can safely eat up to 1,800 calories daily and still take off the pounds gained over a weekend.

Now then—presuming your weight is normal (from *not* having binged over weekends for a while but having stuck to a reducing diet faithfully seven days a week to get to the starting point), you may now begin this low willpower, high-protein diet that allows for binges and slide-backs on weekends, and you may live with it slenderly and healthily forever.

Doesn't this bingeing and reforming wreak havoc with your system? You've heard that going up and down in poundage is bad for you. Says Dr. Blackman, "The gain and subsequent loss of a pound and a half a week isn't extreme enough to hurt you. Furthermore, you probably won't binge *every* weekend. Some Saturdays and Sundays you'll stay with your Monday-through-Friday eating plan and your weight will remain constant."

In suggesting that you follow this plan, we also presuppose that you have no health problem that requires a special diet—and it's recommended that you take a multivitamin pill or pills daily.

Here are the details of Dr. Blackman's plan. The sensible part of the diet—Monday through Friday—is purposely spartan-sounding: no butter on vegetables or bread, nothing but lemon juice on your salad. Dr. Blackman says this is because, "If you give dieters a finger, they'll take a hand, and it's better to start strict." If butter on your bread, cream in your coffee, and salad dressing on your lettuce are *essential* to you, however, you can have them and still stay under 1,000 calories a day by making substitutions. I'll tell you these in a moment.

Since most busy working girls haven't time to prepare low-calorie casseroles or complicated de-calorized desserts, I haven't included them here. You can find recipes for these in cookbooks and some in the last chapter of this book, and substitute them for something else on the list if you like, although it will probably be at the price of less protein and therefore less pep and vitality for you.

To follow Dr. Blackman's plan, each of these must be included in your diet every day: two glasses of skim milk; half a pound of meat, fish, or fowl; one egg; three servings of fruit, preferably fresh. (If canned, the sweetening should be artificial.) One serving of fruit should be fresh oranges or grapefruit. Four servings of vegetables, the less cooked the better. One should be completely raw. One or more should be green, and ideally none will be starchy. Six to eight glasses of water. (Forget the diets that say forget water! You *need* it; keep a jar in the refrigerator cold and handy to sip.)

These foods can be scheduled roughly the following way, although there's nothing to say you can't have broiled fish for breakfast and your egg hard-boiled for lunch:

Breakfast: Fruit—fresh orange or grapefruit slices (just peel off the yellow color and leave some of the white porous skin on for you to eat); one egg fixed your favorite way (enough butter to keep it from sticking to the pan is admissible, but why not try a Teflon pan for butterless cooking?); one slice one-hundred-percent whole-wheat toast; coffee or tea with skim or regular milk if you wish.

Luncheon (or Supper): Lean meat ($\frac{1}{4}$ pound), cottage cheese, or fish; one vegetable; salad of greens with lemon or vinegar; one whole-wheat roll or slice one-hundred-percent whole-wheat bread; fresh fruit; one glass skim milk.

Dinner: Lean meat ($\frac{1}{4}$ pound), fish, or fowl; two vegetables; fresh fruit; one glass skim milk.

Within this framework, there are dozens of different meal combinations possible, considering how many different kinds of meat, fish, fowl, vegetables, and fruit there are. You may also substitute eggs and cheese for meat occasionally and these can be "dreamed up" delicious different ways.

Dr. Blackman points out that the *size of portions* is of utmost importance. "Many women will eat a one-pound porterhouse steak and think it's slimming," he says. "Actually, that much steak contains *at least* 1,180 calories—the equivalent of a whole day's food."

Most women don't like to be bothered with kitchen scales, so Dr. Blackman suggests that when buying ground beef, steak, or veal at the market, you ask the butcher to weigh and wrap it in quarter-pound packages. This eliminates all guesswork. You can eat bigger portions of fish and poultry because they contain fewer calories than meat. For instance, instead of one hamburger patty, you can substitute *half* a broiled chicken, a *whole* medium-sized lobster, *fifteen* shrimp, or *one cup* of crab meat. Roast meats are relatively high in calories—you can have only *one* slice of roast beef, veal, or lamb (and no pork or ham at all).

This diet gives you lots of "outs." For instance, if you must have a teaspoon of butter on your morning toast (35 calories), you can "save up" this amount of calories by sticking to low-calorie vegetables and avoiding the starchy ones. Choose among these vegetables: asparagus, broccoli, Brussels sprouts, cabbage, cauliflower, celery, chicory, cucumber, escarole, greens, lettuce, mushrooms, okra, peppers, radishes, sauerkraut, string beans, summer squash, tomatoes (or tomato juice). Avoid (because of high carbohydrate content): corn, lima beans, parsnips, peas, potatoes.

There is also a drinking diet! If you wish to have two relaxing highballs before dinner, they're allowed. (No more than two, though.) Just skip the glass of skim milk (80 calories) at lunch and dinner. Or you can "save" the fruit and milk from lunch and dinner for midafternoon or midnight snacks.

Most important: You must stick to the diet just outlined Monday *through* Friday night. No cheating. Then Saturday morning, whoopee! Anything goes!

What about the famous diet that presumably lets you eat all the meat you want to and drink all the booze—without adding pounds? Isn't that easier? Dr. Blackman feels no diet that rules certain delicious foods out of your life forever, except in minuscule portions, can possibly be lived with. Also your body needs a *balanced* assortment of foods. The plan outlined here allows you to keep in shape, once you're *down* there, by eating a balanced, satisfying diet through the week and eating *absolutely anything and everything you want* on weekends.

Occasionally you'll find a binge happening to you through the *week*. O.K., you must consider the Tuesday or Wednesday on which it occurs the *weekend* and get busy for the next five days after that making amends. Whenever possible, however, it seems a more satisfying way of life to make weekends consistently *la dolce vita* happy-eating time.

Guilty Monday. All right . . . it's Monday morning and you know you've been a bad, wicked girl. Now you must atone for your indulgence and begin to get that pound and a half of flab off before it has time to solidify into hard, ugly fat. Guilty Monday consists of two activities. One, you must start back on your high-protein, no-nonsense weekday diet without fail. This one day only you might consider skipping the piece of bread or toast at breakfast and lunch, the skim milk at lunch and dinner. (No liquor, of course.) This will save you an extra 360 calories from even your sensible diet, and you'll be off to a raging good start. (Since you probably hate the sight and smell of food and alcohol after the weekend anyway, you won't feel too deprived.) Two, you take extra exercise in painless forms. During lunch you walk . . . to the library, the park, the theater to pick up those tickets you wanted, to a store that's eight blocks away. Sitting at your desk or wherever your daily work is done, do the tummy-sucking-in, six-second breath-holding isometric exercises (see page 130), which tighten muscles. These are in addition to the daily exercise that's part of your regular schedule. To keep up your morale, you may snack midmorning and at bedtime (conscience clear) with any of these: raw vegetables (celery, tomato, radishes, cucumber, lettuce); clear broth or bouillon; artificially sweetened gelatin; hot or iced tea with lemon, or coffee; non-caloric drinks with a wedge of fresh lime or lemon squeezed in. (Ginger ale, lemon, cream, orange, coffee, black cherry, grape, coffee, and cola flavors are all delicious.)

That's all there is to Guilty Monday except that

you're going to concentrate on improving your mind and body instead of thinking about your appetite. You're going to know that it won't be long before you can eat bingefully again—the weekend will be here in no time—provided you succeed in being a good girl for the five days in between.

Other Monday-to-Friday Helps. Work out an exercise plan to follow every day, but let it be a simple one you can live with. *The Royal Canadian Air Force Exercise Plans for Physical Fitness,* which take twelve minutes a day, are excellent. (Mail $.95 plus $.10 handling charge, to Simon & Schuster Mail Order Dept., 1 West 39 Street, New York City, and they'll send the latest edition of the book by Pocket Books.) Perhaps you prefer walking a mile to and from work, or after dinner, playing tennis, swimming, or dancing. If you're lucky enough to have a swimming pool or the use of a friend's, water exercises (see page 161) are excellent. Consistent exercise is part of the plan that lets you binge on weekends.

Why not bring your lunch to work as often as possible? You can bring exactly what you need and not be tempted by the sight and smell of restaurant fare. Think of the *money* you'll save!

Artificial sweetener should always be in your handbag. You may even want to carry your own bottle of lemon or vinegar salad dressing.

If you'll be sitting all evening—at a play, movie, or concert—walk there and back if possible, and no nibbling at intermission!

Before spending the evening watching television, get your "allowable snack" all ready and have it waiting in the icebox—canned mushrooms with capers and tomato slices, or low-calorie grape soda with one slice of canned pineapple floating on top.

Don't skip meals. When you *do* eat, you'll gobble down everything but the silverware.

Don't keep naughty things in the house that you *know* you can't resist. If your husband loves rich desserts, perhaps he'd be good enough to eat them at lunchtime (unless he's on this wonderful high-protein, low willpower plan *with* you, which would be better for him). The children can eat their naughty foods during the week away from home, *too*. No, you do *not* have to bake them batches of triple butter-scotch surprise to have them know you love them.

Take *lessons*—in water-coloring, Yoga, sewing, Italian for your trip abroad next year. Feel virtuous writing to relatives or cleaning out your desk or bureau drawers. Telephone all your friends and have a good gossip. Haven't you noticed that extremely busy and successful people are often more slender than their friends? They're so busy they forget to have false hunger pangs.

Weigh in on Monday morning. Don't keep looking through the week. Stick to 1,000 calories a day Monday through Friday without cheating. Along about Wednesday, peel off your clothes and gaze at yourself in a full-length mirror. You're *beautiful!* Friday night weigh in again. You're where you should be. Saturday and Sunday eat what you please. Isn't it a lovely life!

One man I know has developed another version of self-indulgent diet maintenance. He eats everything, but has the rare talent to push the plate away half-full. For example, at a French bistro he'll order country pâté, smear it on fresh, crusty bread, eat very slowly and appreciatively, but leave more than half of it. Same for the steak au poivre, pommes frites, and chocolate mousse. I admire him as if he were Albert Schweitzer—because *I* could no more leave half a mousse uneaten in its dish than I could drive a space capsule. But if you can restrain yourself, go right ahead and order everything on the menu! You'll never feel lonely for the *tastes* of fattening dishes, can experiment with all varieties exotica, and you won't gain back an ounce.

Apparently this is a *popular* technique. Here's one (female) taste-freak's first-person account of this weight-maintenance method:

"To me, *glamour* is that Gabor girl with her cavernous icebox—empty, except for a dozen orchids and a salami. Cowering in my size eighteen kimono before my bathroom scale or memorizing the latest crash diet—consommé, kelp, and soy beans—I brooded about that salami and those orchids.

"I knew that faced with a dozen orchids and a salami, my willpower would tremble, quiver, and melt away. I would nibble deviled orchid for hors d'oeuvre and puree of orchid as potage, devour the salami as entrée with orchid slaw, and polish off the remaining blossom as dessert. To be brutally frank, there is practically nothing I won't eat.

"But now I have discovered the incredible, intoxicating joy of *tasting*.

"I had company for dinner. And it was traumatic all right—nibbling watercress and one slice of lean beef, 2 by 4 by $\frac{1}{4}$ inches—while everyone else ate stuffed avocado, baked lasagna, and heaps of hot buttered French bread. For dessert my guests ate Baked Alaska while I crept off into the kitchen for dietetic gelatin. I sat there, eyes fixed longingly on the remnants of lasagna and Alaska and something evil seized me. I leaped off the kitchen stool and dug in. I took a heaping spoonful of everything. Yes, everything. Slowly. Everything tasted exactly as I had thought it would—great. But surprisingly enough, I felt great, too. As I joined my guests for coffee, I no longer felt underprivileged or deprived. I scarcely felt like a dieter at all.

"From that day on whenever I found myself dining on something sensible or inedible while hankering for something beyond that day's calorie allowance, I would quell the pangs of martyrdom with a taste of what everyone else was eating—a forkful of fettucini, the peak of a chicken croquette, one sugar-coated bourbon ball, a heaping teaspoonful of butter-pecan ice cream. And if *no one* happened to be eating, I would run to the nearest bakery shop and buy myself a modest treat—one macaroon cookie, or a miniature lemon tart no bigger than a twenty-five-cent piece.

"It is amazing how just one taste buffers up the willpower.

"I didn't suffer as I had before. I am convinced it is suffering that makes for the unsuccessful diet, that makes most dieters quickly put on all the weight they have lost, plus a few pounds. But tasting worked.

Over the months I kept losing—about two pounds a week for an impressive total of twenty-eight pounds.

"Here's how to taste: Next time you dine at the best restaurant in town, order your plain broiled perch and unbuttered spinach but encourage your husband or boyfriend to order the most sour-creamed, butter-drenched rice-mounted delicacy. Then insist on a taste. Also nibble a bit of his chocolate mousse and sip his champagne. If he carries on, you may tell him this is your new diet plan. Or tell your husband you are pregnant again and this is a new sort of craving. Months later when your waistline is reappearing instead of gaining on you—you can explain.

"Or tell your boy friend your psychiatrist thinks you are developing schizophrenic tendencies and wants you to humor them. Or tell him you think someone is trying to poison him and you want to taste everything before it enters his mouth.

"Do not be intimidated by strangers. Cater to your slightest whim. Tell them tasting is a kind of compulsion to you—like shoplifting is to other people. Or hint your behavior is part of a new philosophy—Far Eastern, of course. Say: 'Zen, darling.' Snitch a taste. Munch. Smile enigmatically.

"*Tasting*, you will find, is a science. As a sincere —though indulgent—dieter, there is only so much you can afford to put away each day. Be discriminating. Take that giant baked stuffed potato. Taste the crust, all cheesy and studded with chives. Don't bother with the inside. It's plain old mealy baked potato anyway. Or take lobster—calorically lethal in Newburg or thermidor but practically no calories at all boiled or broiled. Only don't deprive yourself of the butter. That is suffering. But let only the tip of each lobster chunk brush the melted butter. That way you get the taste, the odor, the texture, the flavor, the thrill, and only a smidgen of the calories.

"With *tasting*, there is only one rule. It is: *one taste only.* But there is even an exception to this rule. For as every good cook and amateur glutton knows, there are two kinds of tastes—mandatory and extracurricular. Out in the kitchen, brewing some divine dish for the nondieters in your family, there are times when you absolutely must taste. 'Season to taste,' the recipe will say. In this case, you are permitted one taste as an operational expenditure, and later one of the finished product for sheer pleasure.

"The wonderful thing about *tasting* is that it goes with practically any diet. If your diet simply calls for moderation and counting calories, by all means, tabulate the calories in every *taste*. A cream puff is only 125 calories. So your morsel—even if you can get away with a third—is only 40. A sip of your husband's gin and tonic won't cost more than 20 calories and a bite of his pizza, 40. A modest spoonful of rice pudding, 25, one French-fried potato (2 by $\frac{1}{2}$ by $\frac{1}{2}$ inches), $19\frac{1}{2}$. It's not difficult at all, especially carrying one of the new, more complete, calorie counters. You'll be so busy subtracting, dividing, and multiplying, you won't have time to brood.

"You may become so fond of *tasting*, you will want to give up eating altogether. Then it's called smorgasbord. Limit yourself to 1,000 to 1,500 calories' worth of tastes a day until you reach the weight you have pined so long for. And then boost your tasting allowance gradually till you find the amount that keeps you slim.

"One warning: Don't try tasting with salted nuts. The myth is there is no such thing as eating *one* salted peanut. But the myth is true."

CHAPTER 22: IT'S STILL IN YOUR HEAD

Test: It's Friday evening, 6 P.M. You're in the super-market, and you have absolutely no plans for the weekend. The new man is off skiing with the boys (didn't invite you!), and nobody else in your life has so much as suggested a double feature or a hockey game to fill those empty hours. If you're lucky, Dustin Hoffman may appear on the Tonight Show. If not, life is blank till Monday. Further cluttering that gloomy picture, tomorrow afternoon has to be de-voted to cleaning out your closets. Get the scene? O.K., wheeling your basket around Temptationville, what are you loading up on for these forty-eight hours ahead? If it's chicken breasts, fresh pineapple, and rhubarb, you've *really* changed, deep down in your soul. If it's that *plus* (stuck away in the bottom of the basket) a quart of Swiss-chocolate you-know-what and a frozen devil's-food cake to go with it, your head is still in the wrong place—even though the body's spectacular. You haven't stopped using food for the wrong reasons, just the way you did in your teen-age days or before your recent weight loss.

Chocolate ice cream, even the kind with nuts and bits of marshmallow and chocolate chip laced in, never has and never will replace what you *really* want this weekend, is guaranteed not to soothe the depression or fill the emptiness for more than a few seconds. What's worse, guilt will overtake you ("I've

battled so hard to get where I am, and now. . . .")
You must learn to kill that age-old equation, "Food
equals a panacea for tension/depression/boredom."
Instead of *automatically* filling this bleak weekend
with carbohydrates, why not indulge in nonfood
substitutes? Spend $7.95 on that juicy new bestseller
that you've been dying for but had frugally decided
to wait for in paperback. Go to eleven movies, one
after the other, all junk films that you adore but no
one will ever take you to. Buy some trumpet-blare
print fabric, and make yourself a kicky at-home skirt
or some new throw pillows.

Are you still vulnerable to attacks of midnight-
snack desperation? Are you shocked into a *coma*
because you expected this craziness to vanish with
the fat and it hasn't? Do you loathe yourself today
because you simply had to run out last night, rain-
coat over nightie, for a pound of cashews and a giant
candy bar? The reappearance of those cravings and
compulsions is, unfortunately, a major source of
post-diet disappointment. Don't let them drive your
weight back up the scale. Expect them—you're not
weak and dumb and cuckoo, nor the only recently
reduced human afflicted by this dilemma.

Courage! Thin new you can handle the attacks
in a thin new way. Whatever hidden or surface
anxieties are driving you out into the cold night for a
sweet, why not try being Samson-strong . . . *living*
with them? Instead of tranquilizing your emotions
with food, sit on your couch, stare at the wall, *feel
tense*—and analyze what's going on inside. *Think:*
Is it anger at your parents, sexual frustration, terror
of being fired? What? Can you quell the feelings by
any other means than eating? If you don't try *temporarily* doping yourself with food, you might be able
to banish the problem *totally*.

Perhaps, like me, you've had the experience of
opening a restaurant menu, deciding virtuously on
fillet of lemon sole and green salad, then suddenly
blurting out an order for cream-sauced madnesses
and wolfing down slice after slice of soft bread with
sweet butter. Stop for a minute. Just stop right there
and examine the need that's suddenly taken control
of you. Why am I *really* eating this? Can I avoid it?

If not, can I just nibble and leave half on the plate? How will I feel if I *don't* eat it? What about my new figure? How steep is the price I'm paying for these potatoes?

Crucial in the weight-loss maintenance game: your *flexibility*. Don't panic. *You're* in control now, not your raging appetites. If *you* gain a pound, *you* can remove it. You've done it before.

Now for those fast-fast-fast blitz diets we all love. You've achieved your normal weight, have only to shed a wee few pounds recently picked up. What you mustn't forget is that crash diets are only appropriate for a couple of days, a week at the very *most*, and you should be in perfect health before undertaking any of them. They all lack one or another nutritional requirement for a realistic lifetime diet, so be sure to take a multivitamin tablet each day.

GRAPEFRUIT AND EGGS *(three days, three pounds)*
$\frac{1}{2}$ grapefruit and a hard-boiled egg 4 or 5 times a day

EGGS AND WINE *(three days, three pounds)*
Breakfast: 2 eggs, black coffee (eggs cooked any style)
Lunch: 2 eggs, 4 oz. dry white wine
Dinner: 2 eggs, 8 oz. dry white wine

MILK AND BANANAS *(five days, five pounds)*
6 bananas and 3 glasses of skim milk each day

ICE MILK *(two days, two pounds)*
One quart of vanilla or coffee ice milk each day

SALAD *(seven days, seven to ten pounds)*

Breakfast: ½ grapefruit; ½ cantaloupe, or ½ cup tomato juice or orange juice

Lunch and dinner: vegetable salads, raw or cooked, any amount. No avocado, beans, peas, potatoes. Dressing must be bottled low-calorie at 2 calories per tablespoon, or lemon juice and herbs.

COTTAGE CHEESE AND FRUIT *(two days, two to five pounds)*
For each meal:
1 cup (8 oz.) cottage cheese
3 dietetic canned peach halves, or 7 apricot halves, or 1 orange, or ¾ cup berries
2 squares RyKrisp brushed with butter and cinnamon, toasted under broiler

ASPARAGUS *(two days, two to five pounds)*
For each meal:
Unlimited number of fresh steamed asparagus, with one of the following toppings:
Lemon juice and diet margarine
Low-calorie salad dressing
Grated Parmesan cheese
Poached egg

NIBBLING CRASH *(seven days, four pounds)*
Breakfast: ½ cantaloupe
11 A.M.: 1 hard-boiled egg
Lunch: 3-oz. broiled hamburger, 2 dill pickles
4 P.M.: 1 medium apple
Dinner: ½ cup tomato juice, 6 oz. broiled fish, green salad
11 P.M.: 1 glass skim milk

600-CALORIE-A-DAY BLOCKBUSTER *(two days, four to five pounds)*
First Day
Breakfast:
½ grapefruit
1 slice protein toast with margarine
1 glass skim milk

Lunch:
1 slice protein toast with margarine
2 scallions
1 glass skim milk

1 plum

Dinner:
lettuce with 1 tablespoon low-calorie dressing
1 cup bouillon
6 oysters on the half shell
½ cup boiled zucchini
5 radishes

Second Day
Breakfast:
½ banana
1 slice dry toast
1 boiled egg

Lunch:
¼ cup cottage cheese
5 Saltines

Dinner:
2 broiled or boiled frankfurters
1 cup carrots
½ banana
½ cup vanilla ice cream

On all of these blitz diets, *unlimited* quantities of black coffee, tea, diet soda, and bouillon are allowed. However, don't try the most strenuous ones on work days where energy is pouring out of you.

PART FOUR

THE DIETER'S GOURMET KITCHEN

CHAPTER 24: FOOD HINTS FOR THE SUPER-SUCCESSFUL DIETER

Diet foods don't have to be dreary—but they can be *tricky.* Here are some food-fact tidbits that your mother probably never taught you about low-calorie shopping, cooking, and eating. These tips should become habits—as vital a part of your psyche as those old fattening *hangups* used to be!

1. Make diet meals look as sexy and appetizing as possible. Use smaller plates to disguise the fact that you're eating smaller portions. Decorate food with parsley and lemon slices, paprika, and herbs where appropriate.

2. Keep cut-up raw vegetables in the refrigerator in a covered container of cold water: cucumbers sliced in eighths, radishes, raw turnips, the ubiquitous carrot and celery strips. When you're hungry, they'll be as speedily at hand as a cookie.

3. Beware, beware of teeny additions that creep into your diet: an eyedrop of cream in the coffee, a dab of mayonnaise, a smidgeon of butter. Don't!

4. Learn to leave food on your plate. As your appestat readjusts to normal, pay attention to these brand new voices that whisper, "I'm full." If you can't forget your mother's lectures about the starving children in Asia, send money.

5. Get used to feeling hungry occasionally—a

sensation you've rarely allowed to exist. It's not so bad, and certainly won't kill you.

6. Always remove the skin from poultry, preferably before cooking. Also, try to limit yourself to the white meat.

7. Margarine and butter have the same number of calories. Just because the former contains less saturated fat doesn't mean it's a diet goody to be consumed like celery. But *diet* margarine and *whipped* butter have half the calories of regular versions.

8. Keep a can opener in your desk at the office, alongside several tinned nibblies. (While others are gluttoning on 4 P.M. coffee cake, you have asparagus spears, water-packed tuna, zucchini, dietetic apricots.)

9. Powdered milk is a hundred percent fat free, a better average than container skim milk, and tastes just as good. The secret: Prepare it at night for use the next day.

10. Beware of labels. "Half the fat calories of regular _____" does *not* mean the same as "Half the calories of _____." If you're ever in doubt, consult your Calorie Counter.

11. Learn to love cottage cheese. (It *is* lovable, really it is.) Use it instead of mayonnaise to make tuna salad and egg salad; instead of cream cheese (cottage cheese and dietetic jelly on toast; lox and cottage cheese on half a toasted bagel). Mix it with slices of fresh orange, apple, and pear for a perky lunch; with skim milk and herbs as a raw vegetable dip. Cottage cheese is one of the most *versatile* foods. You don't have to eat that skim-milk version, either—the butterfat content of cottage cheese is so low you can enjoy the creamiest of brands.

12. Eat slowly. Very slowly. Really taste each morsel. (Fat Souls tend not to taste our food, did you know that?) Physiologically, slow eating allows the blood sugar level to rise and satiate your hunger. Psychologically, it makes you believe you're eating more than you really are, is a marvelous means of solving the second-helping trial at dinner parties. ("I'd love some more, but you see I'm only halfway through what's on my plate.") Also, chewing—

slowly, lustfully—is one of the major satisfactions of eating.

13. Drink a lot of water. I mean eight glasses a day. This is a highly underrated diet activity. Water really does fill you up, especially a big glass half an hour before meals.

14. Force yourself, no matter how poignant the pain, to break the coffee-with-milk habit. (The most convincing argument I know for black coffee: If you're at a restaurant or party where they only serve coffee with heavy cream, you'll take it that way and add an unneeded 50 calories to your day's total.) You will definitely grow to adore black coffee (*that's* the *true* taste of coffee, you realize) after two weeks or so.

15. Use dry white or dry red wine in cooking. It transforms a yawn dish into gourmet paradise, and the too-good-to-be-truth is that the alcohol evaporates in the cooking, taking with it almost all of the wine's calories (not true, though, of sweet wines).

16. A general guide to ice cream calories (per cup):

(a) rich in butterfat, expensive   400
(b) ice milk   270
(c) low in butterfat, inexpensive   255
(d) sherbet   240
(e) fruit or water ices   145

(These counts do vary according to flavor and brand.)

One of the boons and glories of dieting is that you needn't live on hamburger alone; truly *sublime* low-calorie dishes—even *feasts*—do exist. (Some may already be among your favorites!) With a gloveful of basic ingredients (the omnipresent bouillon, tomato juice, and a universe of spices), fearless imagination, and the following recipes, you'll create meals lofty enough for "ooo"s and "aaah"s from the most jaded gourmet dinner guests. (Most are also simple enough to make for solo eating.)

APPETIZERS

SUPER CLAM DIP	1 cup cottage cheese 1 7-oz. can minced clams, drained 2 tbsp. minced parsley 1 tsp. grated onion or onion juice Dash salt

Combine all ingredients and beat in blender until fairly smooth. Use as dip for raw vegetables, to stuff celery, to spread on cucumber canapes. Makes $1\frac{1}{2}$ cups.

MARINATED SHRIMP

1 lb. shrimp, washed, de-veined and cooked
1 cup dry white wine
2 tbsp. vegetable oil
2 tbsp. water
3 tbsp. catsup
$\frac{1}{4}$ green pepper, diced
$\frac{1}{2}$ onion, sliced
1 clove garlic, pressed
1 tsp. salt
$\frac{1}{8}$ tsp. red pepper sauce
2 tsp. Worcestershire sauce
$\frac{1}{4}$ cup vinegar
2 tbsp. parsley, chopped
Dash pepper

Bring everything but shrimp to boil and simmer 5 minutes. Add shrimp, cover, remove from heat. Refrigerate. Will keep several days.

EGGPLANT DIP

1 large eggplant
1 onion, finely chopped
1 tomato
Salt, pepper, vinegar, oil

Boil eggplant, then peel. Chop with onion and tomato, adding rest of ingredients to taste. Chill.

218

STEAK TIDBITS

2 lbs. sirloin steak, cut into 1-inch squares
$\frac{1}{2}$ cup soy sauce
$\frac{1}{4}$ cup water
3 tbsp. bourbon
$\frac{1}{4}$ tsp. ginger

Marinate meat in other ingredients for several hours, the last two hours at room temperature. Heat oven to broil. Remove meat from marinade, broil about 3 minutes. Makes 30 bits.

STUFFED MUSHROOMS

16 large mushrooms
1 small onion, minced
$\frac{1}{4}$ cup green pepper, minced
2 tsp. vegetable oil
$\frac{1}{4}$ lb. lean ground round
Salt, pepper
$\frac{1}{4}$ cup tomato juice
$\frac{1}{4}$ tsp. lemon juice

Heat oven to 350°. Mince mushroom stems, sauté with onion and pepper in oil until tender. Stir in beef and cook until it turns brown. Add salt and pepper to taste. Remove from heat and stir in tomato juice and lemon juice. Fill mushroom caps. Bake in 350° oven for about 20 minutes.

TUNA-STUFFED CELERY

1 7-oz. can tuna, water-packed
1 tbsp. grated onion
2 tbsp. minced parsley
1 tbsp. chopped pimento

1 tbsp. oil
Salt, pepper

Soak celery stalks in iced salted water. Drain tuna well. Beat in blender with remaining ingredients. Dry celery stalks and stuff with the mixture. Makes $\frac{3}{4}$ cup.

CRAB MEAT AND WATER CHESTNUT DIP

1 tbsp. soy sauce
6 tbsp. low-calorie mayonnaise
2 tbsp. chopped chives
1 7-oz. can crab meat, drained and flaked
$\frac{1}{2}$ cup water chestnuts, drained and sliced

Mix first 3 ingredients together, then toss with crab meat and water chestnuts. Chill. Makes $1\frac{3}{4}$ cups.

HAM DIP

1 8-oz. can deviled ham
1 hard-boiled egg
1 tbsp. grated onion
$\frac{1}{3}$ cup skim milk
1 pint cottage cheese
$\frac{1}{3}$ cup sliced pimentos, with oil
Salt, pepper

Mash ham and egg together. Add onion, then remaining ingredients.

220

LIVER PÂTÉ

1 lb. chicken livers
3 anchovy fillets
$\frac{1}{2}$ cup dry white wine
$\frac{1}{4}$ tsp. salt
Pinch pepper
$\frac{1}{4}$ cup chopped parsley

Broil livers until lightly browned. Place in bowl, cover with remaining ingredients, and marinate in refrigerator overnight. Pour off half the wine, beat remaining ingredients in blender until smooth. Makes $1\frac{1}{2}$ cups.

SARDINE SPREAD

1 4-oz. can sardines, mashed
$\frac{1}{4}$ cup catsup
$\frac{1}{4}$ cup diet cottage cheese
2 tbsp. onion, minced
2 tbsp. green pepper, chopped
$\frac{1}{2}$ tsp. red pepper sauce
1 tbsp. lemon juice
2 tbsp. parsley, chopped

Combine first 7 ingredients and chill. Garnish with parsley when ready to serve. Spread on melba toast, in celery, or on cucumber or zucchini slices.

SOUPS
(HOT AND COLD)

CURRIED MUSHROOM SOUP

3 tbsp. diet margarine
$\frac{1}{2}$ lb. fresh mushrooms, sliced
1 small onion, sliced
1 tsp. curry powder
1 quart chicken broth (4 bouillon cubes and 4 cups water)
1 cup skimmed milk
Salt, pepper

Melt margarine in saucepan over moderate heat. Add sliced mushrooms and onion. Add curry powder and stir until moisture disappears. Spin in blender with 1 cup of the chicken broth and the milk for 15 seconds. Return to saucepan, add the remaining broth and milk, and heat on low flame for 5 minutes. Season with salt and pepper. Makes 6 servings.

CRAB MADRILENE

2 13-oz. cans consommé madrilene
6 oz. canned crab meat, drained and flaked
Salt, pepper
4 tbsp. dry sherry
6 slices lemon
Fresh parsley, chopped

Heat consommé and crab meat, and season to taste. Remove from heat and add sherry. Serve each cup with a slice of lemon and sprig of parsley. Makes 6 servings.

CUCUMBER SOUP

3 cups plain yogurt
1½ cups finely diced cucumbers
½ cup currants
¾ cup cold water
1½ tbsp. fresh dill weed
3 tbsp. chopped chives
½ tsp. salt
1 tsp. lemon juice
Freshly ground pepper

Beat yogurt for 15 seconds in the blender. Stir in cucumbers and currants. Add water until soup is the consistency of light cream. Add remaining ingredients. Chill well. Makes 6 servings.

GAZPACHO

2 tomatoes, peeled and quartered
1 clove garlic, cut in half
½ green pepper, cut in chunks
½ cup wine vinegar
¼ onion, cut in thick rings
½ carrot, cut in rounds
½ large cucumber, sliced
1 stalk celery, cut in chunks
½ tsp. salt
Pinch pepper
Chopped chives

Blend first 5 ingredients in blender on low speed. When pureed, add next 6 ingredients, being careful not to overflow. Blend first on low, then on high. Chill. Garnish with chives. If you like, you can add more cut-up raw vegetables before serving. Makes a little more than 1 quart.

BEAN SPROUT SOUP

6 cups chicken consommé (preferably College Inn Chicken Broth)
2 cups chopped bean sprouts
3 eggs, beaten
3 tbsp. minced parsley

Heat consommé. Add bean sprouts and simmer about 3 minutes. Remove from heat. Stir in beaten eggs. Sprinkle with parsley. Makes 6 servings.

SEAFOOD STEW

1 large onion, diced
1 medium potato, peeled and diced
1 clove garlic, crushed
3 tomatoes, peeled and chopped
1 bay leaf
2 cups dry white wine
1 quart water
6 peppercorns, crushed
$\frac{1}{2}$ tsp. salt
1 tsp. saffron
$\frac{1}{2}$ green pepper, diced

6 scallions, cut into 1-inch pieces
2 lobster tails, slit (to yield 8 oz. lobster meat)
8 jumbo shrimps, shelled and deveined
½ bunch fresh parsley, chopped
½ lb. halibut or sole, sliced thinly

Bring first 10 ingredients to a boil and simmer, covered, for 1 hour. Add green pepper, scallions, and lobster tails, and simmer another 10 minutes. Then add shrimp and parsley. Simmer 5 minutes, then add halibut or sole. Simmer 5 more minutes. Remove lobster meat from shells, dice, and return to stew. Serve, garnished with additional chopped parsley. Makes 4–6 servings.

FISH AND SEAFOOD

HALIBUT STEAK AU GRATIN

3 tbsp. tomato juice
2 tsp. lemon juice
2 tbsp. white wine vinegar
1 tsp. fresh dill weed
1 tsp. garlic salt
2 lbs. halibut steak
4 tbsp. Parmesan cheese
1 tsp. rosemary leaves
Butter

Mix tomato juice with lemon juice, vinegar, dill, and garlic salt. Put fish in a buttered broiler pan, and pour the sauce over it. Broil, close to flame, 8 minutes, turning once and basting twice. Sprinkle on Parmesan cheese and rosemary leaves, and broil until cheese is melted. Makes 6 servings.

CRAB-SPINACH CASSEROLE

1 package frozen chopped spinach
Dash grated nutmeg
1 cup cottage cheese
$\frac{1}{2}$ onion, diced
$\frac{1}{2}$ cup water chestnuts, drained and sliced
1 7-oz. can crab meat, drained and flaked
$\frac{1}{2}$ cup tomato juice
1 tbsp. lemon juice
2 tsp. soy sauce
Pepper

Cook spinach and drain well. Heat oven to 350°. Mix nutmeg with spinach and spread over bottom of a small, deep casserole. Combine cottage cheese with onion and water chestnuts, and spread over top of spinach. Top with crab meat. Combine remaining ingredients and pour over. Bake 20 minutes. Makes 4 servings.

BAKED STUFFED FILLET

3 cups tomato juice
2 pounds fish fillets
2 cloves garlic, minced
Salt and pepper

Heat oven to 350°. Pour tomato juice into baking pan. Pat fish dry with paper towels, and sprinkle with garlic, salt, and pepper. Top each fillet with one tablespoon of Mushroom-Pepper Stuffing (see following recipe) and roll up carefully, fastening with small toothpicks. Place stuffed fillets one inch apart in pan. Bake 30 minutes, basting frequently. Garnish with lemon wedges if you like. Makes 4 servings.

MUSHROOM-PEPPER STUFFING

2 lbs. fresh mushrooms
1 onion, diced
1½ tsp. salt
2 green peppers, diced
Dash cayenne pepper
2 tbsp. tomato juice

Chop mushrooms and cook in Teflon pan until tender. Add onion, salt, green pepper, and cayenne pepper. Sauté this mixture in tomato juice. Let cool and chop very fine.

227

SHRIMPS AND BROCCOLI

16 jumbo raw shrimps, deveined and washed
1 tsp. sugar
½ tsp. salt
¼ tsp. ginger
1 tbsp. vegetable oil
1 lb. fresh broccoli, heavy stalks only, sliced very thinly
2 tbsp. soy sauce
1 tbsp. sherry
½ cup water
2 scallions, minced

Sauté shrimps, sugar, salt, and ginger in hot oil, stirring constantly until shrimps turn pink. Remove shrimps to heated platter. Add broccoli slices, soy sauce, sherry, water, and scallions to skillet. Simmer, covered, until broccoli is tender but still crisp. Uncover and simmer until liquid evaporates. Return shrimps to skillet, heat through, and serve immediately. Makes 4 servings.

COD PUDDING

1½ cups undiluted evaporated milk
1 tsp. salt
1½ lbs. boneless cod (or haddock)
2 egg whites, beaten stiff

Heat oven to 325°. Place half of milk, salt, and fish in blender and spin for 30 seconds. Stop and scrape sides with spatula. Blend until smooth—about 30 seconds longer. Pour into mixing bowl. Repeat blending with remaining milk, salt, and fish. Lightly fold in egg whites to fish mixture. Pile lightly into greased 1-quart baking dish and bake until pudding is set—about 1 hour. Serve with warmed Mushroom Sauce (see the following recipe). Makes 6 servings.

MUSHROOM SAUCE

1 cup tomato puree
6 oz. chopped broiled mushrooms
2 tbsp. vinegar
$\frac{1}{8}$ tsp. cinnamon
$\frac{1}{8}$ tsp. allspice
$\frac{1}{4}$ tsp. dry mustard
$\frac{1}{4}$ tsp. celery salt
$\frac{1}{2}$ tsp. bottled gravy maker
Artificial sweetener to taste

Blend all ingredients except sweetener until smooth—about 30 seconds. Pour into saucepan, sweeten to taste, and bring to boil. Simmer, uncovered, over low heat 15 minutes. Makes 2 cups.

SCALLOPS IN WINE

24 bay scallops
$\frac{1}{2}$ cup lemon juice
2 tbsp. white wine
8 sliced fresh mushrooms
2 tbsp. chopped shallots
2 tomatoes, peeled and diced
$\frac{1}{2}$ cup clam juice
1 cup chopped parsley

Wash scallops and drain carefully to remove any sand. Preheat broiler 15 minutes. Place the scallops in a heatproof casserole and squeeze lemon juice over them. Broil 2 minutes, shaking to turn juices. Turn scallops, but do not pierce them with a fork. Add wine, then mushrooms, shallots, tomatoes, and clam juice. Cover. Simmer on top of stove 7–10 minutes. Garnish with parsley and serve. Makes 4 servings.

ORIENTAL LOBSTER AND CHICKEN

1 tbsp. diet margarine
1 clove garlic, minced
1 green pepper, sliced in strips
1 small onion, sliced
1 cup celery, diced
1 chicken bouillon cube
$\frac{1}{2}$ cup boiling water
$1\frac{1}{2}$ cups leftover white meat chicken or turkey
1 $6\frac{1}{2}$-oz. can lobster, drained
$\frac{1}{2}$ cup water chestnuts, drained and sliced
2 cups bean sprouts, drained
2 tbsp. soy sauce
$\frac{1}{4}$ tsp. ginger
Pinch pepper

Melt margarine in Teflon skillet. Sauté garlic, green pepper, onion, and celery. Dissolve bouillon cube in water, and add to skillet. Cover, and simmer 8–10 minutes. Add chicken, lobster, and all remaining ingredients, and simmer an additional 5 minutes. Add more water only if necessary. Makes 6 servings.

POACHED HALIBUT WITH DILL SAUCE

$1\frac{1}{2}$ lbs. halibut fillets, cut into 4 pieces
1 tbsp. vegetable oil
3 tbsp. minced onion
$\frac{1}{4}$ cup buttermilk
$\frac{1}{2}$ tsp. onion salt
Pinch pepper

Heat oil in skillet. Sauté onion until limp. Add remaining ingredients, using enough water to bring the pan level up to $\frac{1}{2}$ inch. Cover with aluminum foil, with a small hole for steam cut in the center. Simmer 5–10 minutes, until fish is fork-tender. Serve with Dill Sauce (see the following recipe). Makes 4 servings.

DILL SAUCE

1 large cucumber, grated
1 cup plain yogurt
1 tbsp. lemon juice
$\frac{1}{2}$ tsp. prepared mustard
$\frac{1}{2}$ tsp. dill salt

Combine all ingredients mixing well. Chill.

FILET OF SOLE EN PAPILLOTE

2 pounds of fillets (lemon sole or flounder)
1 tbsp. margarine
$\frac{1}{2}$ lb. mushrooms
1 tbsp. chopped onion
$\frac{1}{4}$ tsp. basil
1 tsp. chopped chives
$\frac{1}{2}$ cup white wine
1 medium tomato, peeled and diced
1 tsp. Worcestershire sauce
Juice of $\frac{1}{2}$ lemon
Dash salt
1 tsp. beurre manie ($\frac{1}{2}$ tsp. butter mixed with $\frac{1}{2}$ tsp. flour)
4 slices peeled lemon

Heat oven to 425°. Rinse and dry the fish and arrange enough for one portion each in center of 4 pieces of aluminum foil. Heat margarine until lightly browned in a skillet. Chop mushrooms and sauté with onions, basil, and chives in the skillet. Add wine to skillet and let simmer until liquid reduces by $\frac{1}{3}$. Add tomato, Worcestershire sauce, and lemon juice. Salt to taste and bring to a gentle boil 4 minutes more. Thicken with beurre manie and divide sauce over the portions of fish. Put a slice of peeled lemon on top of each serving. Seal foil over fish. Bake on cookie sheet for 40 minutes. To serve, snip through foil with scissors on top, turn back foil, and eat right from package. Makes 4 servings.

FISH CURRY

2 tbsp. diet margarine
3 small onions, chopped
2 garlic cloves, chopped
3 tbsp. parsley, chopped
1½ tbsp. grated unsweetened coconut
1½ tsp. turmeric
1 tsp. salt
1½ tsp. curry powder
3 tomatoes, sliced
3 tbsp. plain yogurt
1½ lbs. cod, bass, or trout fillets, cut into small pieces

Sauté onions, garlic, and parsley in hot margarine until lightly browned. Add coconut, turmeric, salt, and curry powder; mix well and cook 3 minutes. Add sliced tomatoes and cook 10 minutes; stir in yogurt and cook 5 more minutes over medium heat. Add fish, cover well with sauce and let simmer, covered, until done (about 10 minutes.) Makes 4 servings.

BEEF

SWEET-AND-SOUR MEATBALLS

3 green peppers
1 lb. ground lean beef
1 tsp. salt
¼ tsp. pepper
1 cup chicken bouillon
1 can Diet Delight apricots
1 tsp. soy sauce
¼ cup vinegar

233

Cut green peppers into eighths; season beef and form into balls the size of a walnut. Brown on all sides in Teflon pan. Remove from pan. Place $\frac{1}{3}$ cup bouillon, apricots with liquid, and green peppers in pan. Cover and simmer 10 minutes. Blend soy sauce and vinegar with remaining bouillon. Add to apricot mixture. Cook slowly, stirring constantly, until thicker. Return meatballs to sauce and cook slowly for 15 minutes. Makes 4 servings.

BEEF IN OYSTER SAUCE

1 lb. top round, cut into 1-inch cubes
1 garlic clove, minced
2 tbsp. vegetable oil
$\frac{1}{4}$ cup soy sauce
$\frac{1}{2}$ cup Chinese oyster sauce (available in any Oriental markets and also many supermarkets)
1 tbsp. cooking sherry
Sugar substitute equal to 1 tsp.
$1\frac{1}{2}$ tsp. bouillon powder or 2 bouillon cubes
$1\frac{1}{2}$ cups hot water
$\frac{1}{4}$ cup mushrooms, chopped
$\frac{1}{4}$ cup water chestnuts, sliced
4 scallions, chopped

Brown meat and garlic in hot oil; add soy sauce, oyster sauce, sherry, sweetener, and bouillon powder mixed with hot water. Cover and simmer 25 minutes. Add mushrooms, water chestnuts, and onion; cook, covered, for 5 more minutes. Makes 4 servings.

STUFFED EGGPLANT

2 small eggplants (about 2 lbs.)
2 tsp. salt
$\frac{1}{2}$ lb. lean ground beef
1 clove garlic, crushed
$\frac{1}{4}$ cup onion, finely chopped
$\frac{1}{4}$ cup green pepper, finely chopped
$\frac{1}{4}$ cup celery, finely chopped
1 can (1 lb.) tomatoes, undrained
$\frac{1}{4}$ tsp. thyme
$\frac{1}{2}$ tsp. Tabasco
$\frac{1}{2}$ cup Grapenuts
$\frac{1}{2}$ cup bread crumbs
$\frac{1}{4}$ cup diet margarine, melted

Wash eggplants, cut in half lengthwise. Add with $\frac{1}{2}$ tsp. salt to 1 inch boiling water in kettle. Simmer, covered, for 15 minutes. Drain and cool. Preheat oven to 375°. Carefully scoop out pulp from eggplant halves, leaving $\frac{1}{4}$-inch-thick shell. Dice pulp, set aside with shells. Sauté beef with garlic until brown. Add onion, green pepper, and celery. Cook over low heat for 5 minutes. Stir in tomatoes, $1\frac{1}{2}$ tsp. salt, thyme, and Tabasco. Remove from heat. Add diced eggplant and the Grape-nuts. Spoon meat mixture into eggplant shells. Place in shallow baking pan. Combine bread crumbs and margarine and sprinkle over stuffed eggplants. Bake, uncovered, about 45–50 minutes, or until hot and bubbly. Makes 4 servings.

WHITE WINE STEW

$2\frac{1}{2}$ lbs. lean round, cubed
2 large onions, diced
1 green pepper, cut in chunks
8 carrots, cut in chunks
6 stalks celery, sliced
2 tsp. salt
1 tsp. rosemary
1 tsp. basil
1 tsp. thyme
2 cups dry white wine
2 cups water
Pepper
Fresh parsley, chopped

Brown meat in Teflon skillet. Remove to stewing pot. Sauté onions and green pepper in skillet. Add to kettle. Add remaining ingredients, except for parsley, and bring to a boil. Cover; simmer slowly $2–2\frac{1}{2}$ hours. Garnish with parsley. Makes 6 servings.

ROAST BEEF SALAD

$\frac{1}{2}$ lb. cooked roast beef
1 medium onion
Lemon juice
1 tbsp. prepared mustard
1 tsp. curry powder

1 tbsp. sugar
Salt, pepper
Juice of $\frac{1}{2}$ lemon
1 cup plain yogurt
Paprika

Trim the roast beef of all fat and cut into matchstick lengths, somewhat thicker than matchsticks. Slice onion thinly and toss with the beef. Sprinkle with lemon juice and let stand in bowl at room temperature 30 minutes. In another bowl mix mustard, curry powder, sugar, salt and pepper to taste, and juice of $\frac{1}{2}$ lemon. Fold this paste into yogurt. Then fold in the meat and onion mixture. Marinate in refrigerator at least 4 hours. Sprinkle top with paprika, serve on bed of lettuce, and garnish with fresh parsley. Makes 4 servings.

STEAK TARTARE

2 pounds very lean ground round steak
2 eggs, beaten
2 tsp. vinegar
2 tbsp. catsup
3 tsp. Worcestershire sauce
4 scallions, minced
4 tbsp. fresh parsley, minced
2 tsp. salt
Pepper
Capers

Combine all ingredients except capers, and toss lightly until mixture is well blended. Chill until ready to serve. Garnish with capers (optional). Makes 4 servings.

POULTRY

CHICKEN AND WATER CHESTNUTS

2 tbsp. diet margarine
1 5-lb. chicken, cut in pieces
2 onions, diced
2 tbsp. tomato paste
1 tsp. paprika
2 tsp. dill weed
1½ cups water
Salt, pepper
½ lb. canned water chestnuts

Melt the margarine in a heavy skillet and sauté the chicken pieces until brown. Remove chicken and sauté onions until brown. Put chicken back, cover, and simmer for 5 minutes. Mix tomato paste with paprika, dill, water, salt and pepper to taste, and add to chicken. Cover and simmer for 1 hour. Then add water chestnuts and cook over low heat 30 minutes or until chicken and chestnuts are tender. Makes 6 servings.

CURRIED CHICKEN

2 15-oz. chicken breasts, split
$\frac{1}{2}$ cup celery, sliced
$\frac{1}{2}$ cup onion, diced
1 clove garlic, minced
$\frac{1}{4}$ cup water
2 apples, unpeeled, diced
$\frac{1}{2}$ lemon, sliced thinly
1–1$\frac{1}{2}$ tbsp. curry powder
2 cups boiling water
3 chicken bouillon cubes
$\frac{1}{2}$ cup seedless green grapes
Sugar substitute to equal 2$\frac{1}{2}$ tsp.

Brown chicken in Teflon skillet. Remove chicken, drain off any fat from the pan. Add celery, onion, and garlic, and cook in $\frac{1}{4}$ cup water until vegetables just start to turn limp. Add apples, lemon slices, and curry powder. Stir and cook 3–4 minutes. Dissolve bouillon cubes in boiling water and add to skillet, along with chicken and remaining ingredients. Cover, and simmer over low heat 40–45 minutes, stirring occasionally. Makes 4 servings.

ORIENTAL BARBECUED CHICKEN

$\frac{1}{4}$ cup soy sauce
1 tbsp. vegetable oil
$\frac{3}{4}$ tsp. dry mustard
$\frac{1}{4}$ tsp. ground ginger
$\frac{1}{8}$ tsp. pepper
1 clove garlic, minced
1 frying chicken, quartered

239

Heat oven to 350°. Mix all ingredients, except chicken. Put chicken in shallow baking pan, and brush on all sides with the mixture. Let stand 30 minutes. Bake 50 minutes, or until tender, turning once or twice and brushing with the sauce. Makes 4 servings.

YOGURT CHICKEN

2 15-oz. chicken breasts, split
$\frac{1}{2}$ cup tomato puree
1 4-oz. can sliced mush-rooms, undrained
$\frac{1}{2}$ onion, finely diced
2 tbsp. fresh chopped parsley
$\frac{1}{2}$ tsp. thyme
1 tsp. salt
Pepper
$\frac{1}{2}$ cup plain yogurt

Brown chicken in Teflon skillet. Drain off fat. Add tomato puree, mushroom liquid (not mushrooms), and next 5 ingredients. Cover, and simmer over low heat 40–45 minutes, until the chicken is tender. Stir occasionally, and add a little water if puree sticks to pan. Add yogurt and mushrooms, stirring until mixture is heated through *but does not boil*. Makes 4 servings.

POULET À L'ORANGE

¼ cup lemon juice
1 cup orange juice
1 tsp. liquid sweetener
1 tbsp. grated orange peel
½ tsp. caraway seeds
¼ tsp. marjoram
¼ tsp. rosemary
1 tbsp. cornstarch
2 lbs. boned chicken breasts, cut in 8 slices

Heat oven to 350°. Combine the two juices. Place next 6 ingredients in saucepan and make a paste with small amount of juice. Add rest of juice. Cook over low flame, stirring constantly until slightly thickened. Place chicken slices in ovenproof casserole and spoon sauce over them. Bake for 15 minutes. Garnish with chopped parsley (optional). Makes 4 servings.

ROAST DUCK WITH CRANBERRIES

½ tsp. ginger
½ tsp. salt
¼ tsp. pepper
¼ tsp. cinnamon
½ tsp. Worcestershire sauce
3 tbsp. diet margarine
1 4½–5 lb. duck, cleaned
2 cups fresh cranberries
Rind of 1 orange, grated (save the juice)
⅓ cup lemon juice
2 tbsp. brown sugar
⅓ cup port wine
1 6-oz. can mandarin orange sections
6 sprigs of parsley

Heat oven to 325°. Mix spices and Worcestershire sauce with margarine, and rub duck with them inside and out. Place duck breast-side up in shallow roasting pan in oven, and roast for 30 minutes. Meanwhile, put cranberries, orange gratings and juice, lemon juice, brown sugar, and wine in a pot and cook until berries are tender. Remove duck from oven and pour off fat. Stuff cavity with cranberries and $\frac{1}{2}$ of the liquid. Replace duck on rack and pour remaining liquid over. Roast for 1 more hour. Baste frequently. Duck is done when leg joint moves easily. Garnish with parsley sprigs and mandarin orange sections. Makes 6 servings.

VEAL

DANISH VEAL ROAST

1 4-lb. boned and rolled veal rump roast
3 tbsp. vegetable oil
2 cups plain yogurt
1 package onion soup mix
3 tsp. fresh dill
1 tsp. onion salt
$\frac{1}{4}$ tsp. pepper

Brown roast in hot oil over medium-high flame. In bowl, combine remaining ingredients and spoon over roast. Cover pan and simmer over low heat $2\frac{1}{2}$ hours, until veal is tender. Makes 6–8 servings.

VEAL SCALLOPS

2 lbs. thinly sliced veal scallops
2 tbsp. vegetable oil
Salt, pepper
1 tbsp. fresh tarragon or $1\frac{1}{2}$ tsp. dried
$\frac{1}{2}$ cup dry white wine
1 tbsp. cornstarch

Pound veal with meat-tenderizing hammer until paper thin. Rub meat well with oil. Let stand at room temperature for 1–2 hours. Preheat Teflon skillet, add veal, a few scallops at a time. Brown quickly on all sides. Return all veal to skillet, and sprinkle with salt, pepper, tarragon, and $\frac{1}{4}$ cup wine. If necessary, add a little water to just cover the meat. Lower heat and continue cooking, turning scallops once. When meat is tender, remove veal to hot platter. Add cornstarch and remaining wine to pan, raise the heat, and cook rapidly 1 minute. Pour juices over veal. Makes 6 servings.

VEAL CHOPS BALKAN

2 tsp. vegetable oil
4 thick veal chops
1 medium onion, chopped
1 clove garlic, minced
3 carrots, sliced
2 medium tomatoes, peeled and diced
1 tsp. salt
$\frac{1}{8}$ tsp. pepper
$\frac{1}{4}$ tsp. rosemary
$\frac{1}{3}$ cup dry white wine
1 can sliced mushrooms, drained

Heat oil and sauté chops until brown on both sides. Add seasonings, wine, and all vegetables except mushrooms. Cover and simmer about 40 minutes, until chops are tender. Add mushrooms, heat 5 minutes. Makes 4 servings.

BROCCOLI-STUFFED VEAL BIRDS

4 slices veal scallops, $\frac{1}{4}$-inch thick
Salt, pepper
Grated rind of 1 lemon
4 broccoli spears
1 can (10–12 oz.) condensed chicken broth
$1\frac{1}{2}$ tbsp. tomato paste
Fresh chopped parsley

Season veal slices lightly with salt and pepper. Sprinkle with lemon rind. Place a raw broccoli spear on top of each. Roll up and fasten with toothpick. Combine chicken broth and tomato paste in a pan. Bring to boil and simmer 5 minutes. Add veal rolls, cover, and simmer 15–20 minutes or until veal is tender. Remove toothpicks. Sprinkle rolls with parsley. Makes 4 servings.

VEAL RAGOUT

1 lb. veal shoulder, cut into 1-inch cubes
2 tsp. diet margarine
3 onions, 2 cut in quarters and 1 cut into thin slices
3 tbsp. lemon juice
$1\frac{1}{2}$ cups hot water
$\frac{1}{2}$ tsp. salt
$\frac{1}{2}$ tsp. rosemary leaves
$\frac{1}{8}$ tsp. cayenne pepper
$\frac{1}{8}$ tsp. black pepper
2 medium carrots, cut in chunks
1 medium green pepper, thinly sliced
1 cup sliced mushrooms
2 tbsp. tomato paste
Chopped fresh parsley

Brown veal slowly in margarine over medium heat. When nearly browned, add thinly sliced onion. Cook until onion is transparent, stirring onion frequently. When meat is browned, add lemon juice and hot water. Scrape sides of pan and blend liquids well. Add spices and simmer, covered, for $1\frac{1}{2}$ hours, adding more hot water if necessary. Add carrots, green pepper, mushrooms, and quartered onions. Simmer, covered, until vegetables are tender. Stir in tomato paste. Garnish with parsley. Makes 4 servings.

VEAL PARMESAN

1 lb. veal, cut into ½-inch-
  thick slices
3 tbsp. diet margarine
1 garlic clove, chopped
⅓ cup tomato paste
3 tbsp. water
2 tbsp. lemon juice
4 tbsp. grated Parmesan
  cheese
Salt, pepper

Heat oven to 325°. Pound veal very thin with a meat-tenderizing hammer. Sauté garlic in margarine in skillet. Add veal, brown slightly on both sides. Place veal and sauce from skillet in baking dish. Cover with blend of tomato paste, water, and lemon juice and sprinkle cheese, salt, and pepper on top. Bake for 20 minutes, until cheese has melted. Makes 4 servings.

LAMB

STUFFED CABBAGE

1 large cabbage
1½ lbs. ground lamb
3 tbsp. tomato paste
1½ tsp. salt
1 clove garlic, pressed
¼ cup uncooked rice
1 tbsp. dried mint, crushed
Juice of 1 lemon

Remove core from the cabbage and place cabbage in kettle of boiling water. Cover, and steam until leaves are easily removed. Drain and cool. Mix meat, tomato paste, $\frac{1}{2}$ tsp. salt, garlic, and rice; blend. Carefully separate cabbage leaves. Place 1 tbsp. of meat mixture on each leaf and roll up. Arrange in heavy casserole, add water to cover, add 1 tsp. salt and mint to water. Weight down with inverted dish. Cover and boil 30 minutes, or until rolls are tender. Remove, sprinkle with juice from 1 lemon, and serve. Makes 6 servings.

LAMB SHANKS

6 lamb shanks
$\frac{1}{2}$ clove garlic, diced
1 tsp. salt
$\frac{1}{2}$ tsp. pepper
1 tsp. paprika
2 tbsp. vegetable oil
1 cup water
1 bay leaf
2 whole peppercorns
1 tbsp. grated lemon rind
$\frac{1}{2}$ cup lemon juice
1 lemon, cut in wedges

Make small cuts in lamb, and insert a piece of garlic in each. Season with salt, pepper, and paprika. Brown slowly in oil in heavy skillet. Add 1 cup water and remaining ingredients, except lemon wedges. Bring to boil, cover, and simmer

2–2½ hours, or until meat is very tender. Turn meat occasionally and baste. Serve with lemon wedges. Makes 4 servings.

MINT LAMB CHOPS

4 large loin lamb chops
4 slices of orange, with rind
4 slices onion
½ cup Blender Mint Sauce (see following recipe)

Broil chops until browned on one side. Turn, broil 30 seconds, top with orange and onion slices. Continue broiling until done. Serve with Blender Mint Sauce. Makes 4 servings.

BLENDER MINT SAUCE

⅔ cup water
⅓ cup fresh mint leaves
2 tbsp. lemon juice
2 tsp. cornstarch
Sweetener to equal 1½ tbsp. sugar
Salt
½ tsp. grated lemon rind

Put water and mint leaves in blender and blend on high speed until mint is very fine. Pour into saucepan. Bring to boil and remove from heat. Dissolve cornstarch in lemon juice; add to pan. Return to low heat, stirring, until mixture reaches boil. Remove from heat, add remaining ingredients. Makes ⅔ cup.

CREOLE LAMB CHOPS

6 shoulder lamb chops, fat trimmed off
1 onion, chopped
$\frac{1}{4}$ cup green pepper, chopped
1 tsp. vegetable oil
2 cups canned tomatoes, drained
$\frac{1}{8}$ tsp. cayenne pepper
$\frac{1}{4}$ tsp. chili powder
1 tsp. salt

Heat oven to 350°. Brown lamb chops well on both sides in Teflon skillet, and place in baking dish. Sauté onion and green pepper in hot vegetable oil. Add remaining ingredients, mix, and simmer for 5 minutes. Pour over lamb chops and bake, covered, for 1 hour. Makes 6 servings.

SALADS

CUCUMBERS IN YOGURT

6 medium cucumbers
1 tbsp. salt
$1\frac{1}{2}$ cups plain yogurt
Salt, pepper
1 tbsp. chopped chives

Peel cucumbers, split them lengthwise, then scoop out seeds with a small spoon, and slice as thinly as possible. Sprinkle slices with 1 tbsp. salt, put them in a

249

bowl, and chill for 1 hour. Place cucumbers between dry towels and press out water. Return to bowl, add yogurt, salt and pepper to taste, and mix well. Sprinkle with chives. Makes 6 servings.

SPINACH AND BACON SALAD

1 lb. raw fresh spinach
$\frac{1}{4}$ small Bermuda onion, minced
5 strips bacon, cooked and crumbled
Bottled vinaigrette or low-calorie Italian dressing
1 hard-boiled egg, grated

Wash spinach well and cut off stems with scissors. Don't break leaves. Toss with onion, bacon and vinaigrette dressing or low-calorie Italian dressing. Sprinkle grated egg on top. Makes 6 servings.

WALDORF SALAD

1 apple, diced
1 cup diced celery
$\frac{1}{4}$ cup crushed pineapple
$\frac{1}{4}$ cup grated carrots
Juice of 1 lemon
$\frac{1}{4}$ cup creamed cottage cheese
$\frac{1}{4}$ cup chopped walnuts
1 tsp. maraschino juice from cherries

Combine first 5 ingredients. Add cottage cheese, nuts,

and maraschino juice. Mix and chill well. Makes 4 servings.

MARINATED ASPARAGUS

1 cup tomato juice
2 cloves garlic, diced
½ tsp. salt
1 tsp. fresh dill
Pepper
4 tbsp. lemon juice
1 lb. fresh asparagus, steamed and chilled
1 cucumber, diced

Mix tomato juice, garlic, salt, dill, pepper, and lemon juice in a bowl. Pour over asparagus spears and top with diced cucumber. Chill 3 hours. Makes 4 servings.

SPICY BEAN SALAD

3 cups sliced snap beans, cooked
1 cup yogurt
2 tbsp. chopped black olives
1 canned pimento, chopped
1 tbsp. prepared mustard
1 tsp. capers, chopped
½ tsp. salt or garlic salt
¼ tsp. marjoram
3 hard-boiled eggs, quartered

Drain beans and blend with all ingredients. Chill for at least 30 minutes. Garnish with 3 hard-boiled eggs in quarters, if you like. Makes 6 servings.

CARROT SALAD

1 large carrot
½ cup crushed pineapple
⅓ cup plain yogurt
2 tsp. fresh orange juice
⅓ cup raisins

Peel and shred carrot. Combine with remaining ingredients and chill well. Makes 4 servings.

TOMATO AND ONION SALAD

4 large tomatoes
1 Bermuda onion
Bottled vinaigrette or low-calorie Italian dressing
1 tsp. fresh dill
½ tsp. basil

Slice tomatoes into rings. Slice red onion into rings and place on top of tomato slices on platter. Add vinaigrette dressing or low-calorie Italian dressing. Sprinkle dill and basil over salad. Chill. Serves 6.

COLE SLAW

5 cups shredded cabbage
1 tbsp. honey
1 tsp. salt
½ tsp. dry mustard
¼ tsp. black pepper
¼ cup green pepper, minced
¼ cup raw carrots, shredded
¼ cup pimentos, diced
½ tsp. grated onion
2 tbsp. salad oil
⅓ cup cider vinegar

Just before serving: toss cabbage with next 8 ingredients. Combine salad oil and vinegar and pour over slaw. Toss well. Makes 6 servings.

VEGETABLES

MUSHROOMS PARMESAN

12 large mushrooms
$\frac{1}{4}$ cup minced onion
2 tbsp. green pepper, minced
$1\frac{1}{2}$ tsp. olive oil
$1\frac{1}{2}$ tbsp. grated Parmesan cheese
$1\frac{1}{2}$ tsp. fresh bread crumbs
Salt, pepper

Heat oven to 375°. Clean mushrooms and chop stems very fine. Sauté onion and green pepper in oil until just tender. Add mushroom stems and cook 5 minutes. Combine mixture with remaining ingredients and stuff mushroom caps. Place in baking dish, and bake for 15 minutes. Makes 4 servings.

DUTCH APPLES AND BEETS

12 oz. beets, sliced
$\frac{1}{3}$ cup onion, chopped
4 tart apples, peeled and chopped
$\frac{3}{4}$ tsp. liquid sweetener

1½ tsp. nutmeg
Salt, pepper
6   tbsp. vinegar

Combine all ingredients but vinegar in a saucepan and simmer, covered, 1 hour or until the mixture becomes pulp. Add vinegar and stir. Remove from heat, mash very finely, and serve. Makes 4 servings.

RATATOUILLE

1   eggplant, peeled and cubed
6   medium zucchini, sliced
1½ onions, diced
2   tbsp. fresh parsley, chopped
2   cloves garlic, pressed
2   tsp. salt
2   tsp. oregano
3   cups canned tomatoes
Pepper
½   cup grated Parmesan cheese

Heat oven to 375°. Cook eggplant and zucchini in boiling, salted water for 5 minutes. Remove and drain. Arrange them in bottom of large, shallow baking dish. Sprinkle onions and parsley. Add rest of ingredients except cheese to the tomatoes, mix well, and pour over. Sprinkle with cheese. Bake 30 minutes until cheese is lightly browned. Makes 8 servings.

254

PINEAPPLE-GLAZED CARROTS

$\frac{1}{2}$ cup water-packed
   crushed pineapple
$\frac{1}{2}$ cup water
1 tsp. liquid sweetener
2 tsp. cornstarch
$\frac{1}{4}$ tsp. salt
1 tsp. diet margarine
1 lb. carrots, freshly cooked
Fresh mint sprigs

Put pineapple and water in saucepan. Stir in sweetener, cornstarch, and salt. Cook over high heat until mixture boils, stirring constantly. Add margarine. Mix with carrots right before serving. Garnish with mint. Makes 4 servings.

SPINACH SOUFFLÉ

1 10-oz. package frozen
   chopped spinach
2 tsp. diet margarine
1 tbsp. flour
Salt
$\frac{1}{2}$ tsp. onion salt
Dash nutmeg
2 eggs, separated

Heat oven to 350°. Cook spinach according to directions. Drain well, reserving $\frac{1}{2}$ cup broth. Melt margarine and stir in flour. Gradually stir in spinach broth and cook, stirring constantly, over medium heat until mixture thickens. Blend in spinach and seasonings, tasting for salt. Beat egg yolks and stir in. Beat whites until stiff and fold into mixture. Pour into greased baking dish, cover, and place in pan of hot water. Bake for about 30 minutes. Remove cover, increase heat to 375°, and bake 10 more minutes or until soufflé is firm. Serve immediately. Makes 4 servings.

SAUCES

FRENCH DRESSING

$\frac{1}{2}$ cup tomato juice
$\frac{1}{2}$ cup vinegar
$\frac{1}{4}$ tsp. dry mustard
Pinch oregano
$\frac{1}{8}$ tsp. garlic powder
6 drops liquid sweetener
Salt and pepper to taste

Combine all ingredients and shake well. Keep refrigerated. Makes 1 cup.

BARBECUE SAUCE

1 tbsp. catsup
1 tbsp. soy sauce or
  Worcestershire sauce
2 dashes Tabasco
Pepper
$\frac{1}{2}$ tsp. salt
$\frac{1}{2}$ cup dry red wine

Combine all ingredients. Beat to blend. Makes $\frac{2}{3}$ cup.

SOUR CREAM | 1 cup diet cottage cheese
$\frac{1}{4}$ cup buttermilk
$\frac{1}{4}$ tsp. lemon juice
Salt

Combine all ingredients and beat in a blender until smooth. Chill at least 4 hours before serving. Makes $1\frac{1}{4}$ cups.

HORSERADISH SAUCE | Prepare the previous recipe for sour cream and add 1 tbsp. horseradish.

SWEET-AND-SOUR SAUCE | $\frac{1}{2}$ cup water
3 tbsp. catsup
3 tbsp. soy sauce
Sugar substitute to equal 3 tbsp. sugar
$1\frac{1}{2}$ tbsp. vinegar
2 tbsp. cold water
1 tbsp. cornstarch

Combine water, catsup, soy sauce, sweetener, and vinegar in a 1-quart saucepan. Heat. Combine cold water and cornstarch. Add to sauce, cooking and stirring until thick and clear. Makes 1 cup.

CHEESE SAUCE | $\frac{1}{4}$ pound farmer cheese
$\frac{1}{3}$ cup buttermilk
1 egg yolk
1 tbsp. lemon juice
$\frac{1}{4}$ tsp. paprika
Salt, pepper

257

In top of double boiler, melt cheese with buttermilk. Add egg yolk and stir until well blended. Add lemon juice, paprika, salt and pepper. Great over any vegetable. Makes 1 cup.

SAUCE VINAIGRETTE

$\frac{1}{4}$ cup vinegar
$\frac{1}{8}$ tsp. paprika
$\frac{1}{2}$ tsp. herbs (dill, tarragon, rosemary, thyme)
1 clove garlic, diced
2 tbsp. water
$\frac{1}{4}$ tsp. liquid sweetener

Combine all ingredients in a tightly closed jar. Refrigerate. Shake well. The flavor improves with age.

WHIPPED YOGURT DRESSING

$\frac{1}{4}$ cup onion, diced
$\frac{1}{2}$ clove garlic, diced
$\frac{1}{4}$ cup celery leaves
1 tsp. salt
$\frac{1}{4}$ tsp. liquid sweetener
1 tbsp. tomato paste
1 cup plain yogurt

Combine all ingredients in electric blender until smooth—about 1 minute. Pour over green salad. Makes 1$\frac{1}{2}$ cups.

MARINADE FOR BROILED MEAT

1 cup dry red wine
½ cup tarragon vinegar
1 tsp. salt
1 tsp. dry mustard
1 bay leaf
6 peppercorns
6 cloves
1 sliced onion
1 clove garlic
1 stalk celery, chopped

Enclose meat and marinade in a plastic bag on a plate in the refrigerator. Marinate 24 hours, turning several times.

DESSERTS

BAKED APPLE

4 medium baking apples
2 packets sugar substitute
Cinnamon
½ bottle low-calorie ginger ale or lemon soda

Preheat oven to 350°. Core apples by piercing center with potato peeler and cleaning out pits and pulp. Sprinkle sweetener and cinnamon through hole in center and over apple. Place in baking dish. Pour soda in dish. Bake for 45 minutes to 1 hour, until apple is tender, basting occasionally. Serve with some diet "whipped cream"—

skimmed milk put through blender with ice cubes, dash vanilla, and artificial sweetener until very thick. Makes 4 servings.

CHOCOLATE SOUFFLÉ

$\frac{7}{8}$ cup skimmed milk
2 tsp. cornstarch
$\frac{1}{4}$ cup cocoa, sifted
Sugar substitute to equal $\frac{1}{2}$ cup sugar
Salt
4 egg yolks, beaten
1 tsp. vanilla
4 egg whites, at room temperature
$\frac{1}{4}$ tsp. cream of tartar

Combine first 5 ingredients in top of double boiler. Cook, stirring constantly, over simmering water until mixture thickens slightly (for about 8–10 minutes). Remove from heat, and beat a little into beaten egg yolks. Pour yolk mixture back into top of double boiler, and cook 3–4 minutes, stirring constantly. Remove from heat, add vanilla, and cool. Heat oven to 325°. Beat egg whites and cream of tartar until very stiff and fluffy, but not dry. Carefully fold in chocolate mixture. Pour into 1½–2-quart soufflé dish. Place in pan with about ½ inch water and bake 40–45 minutes. Serve at once. Makes 6 servings.

BANANA WHIP

1 banana, sliced
1 tsp. lemon juice
1 egg white, unbeaten
Salt
12 drops liquid sugar-sub-
    stitute
$\frac{1}{2}$ tsp. vanilla
Cinnamon or nutmeg

Mash banana with lemon juice; add remaining ingredients except cinnamon or nutmeg. Beat in electric mixer until light and fluffy. Divide into 2 sherbet glasses, and sprinkle with some cinnamon or nutmeg. Serve at once. Makes 2 servings.

PEACHES FLAMBEAU

4 cups water-packed
    peaches
Liquid sugar-substitute to
    taste
1 tbsp. cornstarch
2 tbsp. brandy, heated

Drain water from peaches and add sweetener to taste. Thicken slightly with cornstarch. Pour into saucepan and cook until clear, stirring constantly. Cook peaches in mixture until heated through. Remove and arrange in chafing dish or baking dish, cavity side up. Pour sauce over peaches. Add heated brandy, ignite carefully, and serve flaming. When flames die, spoon the peaches into dessert glasses.

ANGEL FOOLS CAKE

1 cup sifted cake flour
¾ cup sugar
10 egg whites
1 tsp. cream of tartar
¼ tsp. salt
½ tsp. vanilla
½ tsp. almond extract

Heat oven to 375°. Combine the flour with 4 tbsp. of the sugar. Beat the egg whites with cream of tartar and salt until thickened and foamy. Add remaining sugar 1 tbsp. at a time. Continue to beat until egg whites are stiff and fluffy peaks. Beat in vanilla and almond extracts. Sift flour, 2 tbsp. at a time, over the egg whites, folding gently. Pour into 9 or 10-inch pan. Bake for 35–40 minutes or until it springs back when you touch it. Remove pan from oven and invert on wire rack. Let stand as is for at least 1 hour. Then remove cake carefully, running spatula around the edge to loosen.

APRICOT BAVARIAN

4 tsp. unflavored gelatin
¼ cup cold water
1 1-lb. can dietetic apricots
1 tbsp. lemon juice
2 tsp. liquid sweetener
1 cup nonfat dry-milk solids
1 cup ice water

Soften gelatin in cold water. Dissolve over boiling water. Cook apricots until mushy, then strain. Add to gelatin, with lemon juice and sweetener. Cook for 5 minutes. Chill until consistency of unbeaten egg whites. Beat milk solids with ice water until stiff. Fold into gelatin. Chill in 8-cup mold. Makes 12 servings.

PUMPKIN CUSTARD

$1\frac{1}{2}$ cups canned pumpkin
$1\frac{1}{2}$ cups skimmed milk
2 eggs
2 tsp. brown sugar
$\frac{1}{2}$ tsp. vanilla
1 tsp. cinnamon
$\frac{1}{2}$ tsp. ginger
$\frac{1}{4}$ tsp. salt

Heat oven to 350°. Mix all ingredients together well. Pour mixture into 6 custard cups. Bake for 1 hour or until knife comes out clean. Makes 6 servings.

RHUBARB AND STRAWBERRIES

2 lbs. fresh rhubarb
Artificial sweetener
Dash honey
1 lb. fresh strawberries

Wash rhubarb well. Cut off leaves, and chop in chunks. Boil $\frac{1}{4}$ cup water, and simmer rhubarb with sweetener to taste until fruit is mushy. Chill well. Serve with strawberries and dash of honey. Serves 6.

APPLESAUCE MOUSSE

1 cup dietetic applesauce
1 tsp. grated lemon rind
2 tsp. lemon juice
$\frac{1}{4}$ tsp. cinnamon
Pinch of ginger
$\frac{1}{4}$ tsp. vanilla
Sugar substitute to equal 2–3 tbsp. sugar
3 egg whites, at room temperature
$\frac{1}{8}$ tsp. cream of tartar

Combine first 7 ingredients. Beat egg whites and cream of tartar until stiff but not dry. Fold in applesauce mixture. Chill. Serve within 2–4 hours. Serves 4.

AMBROSIA

1 cup plain yogurt
$\frac{1}{4}$ cup raisins
$\frac{1}{4}$ cup blanched walnuts
$\frac{1}{4}$ cup shredded coconut
2 cups unsweetened applesauce
$\frac{1}{4}$ tsp. cinnamon

Blend all ingredients with rotary beater. Pour into individual parfait glasses. Top with additional cinnamon and refrigerate for 2 hours. Makes 6 servings.

DR. ROBERT ATKINS'S DIET CHEESECAKE

8 oz. farmer cheese or pot cheese
2 tsp. vanilla extract
3 packages of Sweet 'N Low sugar substitute

1 oz. Louis Sherry Dietetic
   Pineapple Jam
2 eggs

Heat oven to 350°. Mix all
together except for the
eggs; fold eggs into other
mixed ingredients. Bake
for approximately 20 min-
utes or until slightly hard
on top. Remove; cool;
refrigerate.

INDEX